THE SMALL FLUTE CONCERTO
IN EARLY EIGHTEENTH-CENTURY LONDON

Douglas MacMillan

ISBN 978-1-912271-46-7

Published by Peacock Press, 2019
Scout Bottom Farm
Mytholmroyd
Hebden Bridge HX7 5JS (UK)

Design and artwork by DM Design and Print

Contents

Figures, tables, and music examples

Preface

The act of performing the English small flute concerti over a period of over thirty years, alongside a degree of intellectual scepticism regarding the role of soprano (descant) recorders in the eighteenth century in comparison with the twentieth century, prompted my study of small recorders and their repertoire. During the second and third decades of the eighteenth century, concerti were written in London for 'small flutes', strings and continuo. The word 'flute' at this period implied recorder, and the 'small' or 'little' flutes of the concerti included the sixth flute in d" and the fifth flute in c", the latter of which we now know as the soprano or descant recorder. It is perhaps not always appreciated — because of the all-pervading popularity of the soprano recorder in the twentieth and twenty-first centuries — that few composers of the high Baroque era used the instrument and the assigned repertoire for small recorders in the eighteenth century is far from extensive.[1] The sopranino recorder, sixth and fifth flutes are all 'octave' instruments, sounding above the normal treble instruments such as the alto recorder, the flute, the oboe, and the violin, with the sopranino being the recorder equivalent of the transverse piccolo. The alto recorder predominated from the final quarter of the seventeenth century well into the eighteenth and the vast majority of recorder music was composed for that instrument, both in England and on Continental Europe. Of particular note, European composers tended to write their recorder concerti for the alto, although Vivaldi's three concerti for the sopranino form a notable exception.[2] The use of fifth and sixth flutes in the concerto repertoire is a peculiarly English phenomenon which has received but little attention in the literature of the recorder and, having performed a number of these works, I determined to study more about their history, their composers, their structure and contemporary performance practice and to place them in an historical perspective relating to the recorder and its repertoire within the context of London of the second and third decades of the eighteenth century.

My thanks are due to the late Jeanne Dolmetsch, who introduced me to Baston's second concerto many more years ago than I care to remember, and for allowing me access to material in the Dolmetsch Library at Haslemere. My gratitude is due also to Isobel Clarke and Fiona Smith, two scholarly recorder-playing friends, for their advice and encouragement. Finally, I wish to thank my colleagues in my ensemble Camerata Oriana for accompanying me in the performance of these charming concerti.

---

1   Douglas MacMillan, 'The Descant Recorder in the Early Eighteenth Century' *Recorder and Music*, 7/1, (1981), 12–13.

2   RV 443, 444, 445; there is some evidence that RV443 and 445 may have been performed on the soprano recorder. See Frederico Maria Sardelli, *Vivaldi's Music for Flute and Recorder*, trans.by Michael Talbot (Aldershot: Ashgate, 2007), pp.195–196.

Chapter 1

Preliminary discourse

1.1. Abstract of the chapter

This chapter serves to introduce the topic, with a review of the literature relating to small flute concerti. The London musical scene and performance venues are discussed, together with financial matters relating to salaries, the payments to performers, and the price of theatre tickets. Comments are made on matters relating to amateur performance and gender issues and final paragraphs note the lacunae in the current literature and how these will be filled by the present monograph.

1.2. Introduction

By the early eighteenth century, the term 'concerto' was generally applied to a musical composition contrasting an instrument (or group of instruments) with an accompanying orchestral ensemble. In the case of the English small flute (recorder) concerti, the solo instrument was a fifth or sixth flute (or two sixth flutes), contrasted with a string ensemble (of variable composition) and an accompanying keyboard instrument. The seventeen extant small flute concerti by William Babell, John Baston, Robert Woodcock and Charles Dieupart were composed between *c*.1710 and 1729, but the larger-scale F major concerto by Guiseppe Sammartini probably dates from the 1730s. In addition to the concerti, an anonymous suite in A for sixth flute and strings of English origin will be included in the discourse.

There is no in-depth commentary in the current literature concerning the small flute concerti, and the standard texts contain only scant information on the pieces; whilst acknowledging their existence, they do not apply a critical analysis.[3] Of earlier texts, Christopher Welch, in the second of his *Six Lectures on the Recorder* (delivered in 1898, but only published in 1911) was the first author at the time of the revival of the recorder to refer to the concerti by Babell and Woodcock in an extended footnote to his second lecture.[4] Richard Griscom and David Lasocki's *The Recorder. A Research and Information Guide* discusses several articles which will be cited in the course of the present text, but Lenz Meierott's otherwise comprehensive monograph *Die kleinen Flötentypen* of 1974 fails to mention the concerti.[5] A superficial account of the small flute concerti is given in my article in *The Consort* of 2006, but no critical commentary is given.[6] More specialised articles will be cited and discussed in the appropriate chapters of this volume. Apart from Zöe Franklin's paper on William Babell's sixth flute concerti, there is no account of the harmonic structure of the small flute concerti, and this matter will occupy the third chapter of the present volume.[7] Their orchestration has been

---

3   David Lasocki and Anthony Rowland-Jones in *The Cambridge Companion to the Recorder*, ed. by John Mansfield Thomson (Cambridge: Cambridge University Press, 1995), pp109–110; Edgar Hunt, *The Recorder and Its Music* (Hebden Bridge: 3rd., edn, Peacock Press, 2002), pp.59-60; David Lasocki. "Recorder".*Grove Music Online. Oxford Music Online.* Oxford University Press, accessed 13 July 2017, http://www.oxfordmusiconline.com/subscriber/article/grove/music/23022.

4   Christopher Welch, *Six Lectures on the Recorder and other Flutes in Relation to Literature* (London: Oxford University Press, 1911), n4, pp.150–3.

5   Richard Griscom and David Lasocki, *The Recorder. A Research and Information Guide* (New York: 3rd. edn, Routledge, 2012); Lenz Meierott, *Die geschichtliche Entwicklung der kleinen Flötentypen und ihre Verwendung in der Musik des 17.und 18.Jahrhunderts* (Tutzing: Schneider, 1974).

6   Douglas MacMillan, 'The Small Flute Concerto in 18th-Century England', *The Consort*, 62 (2006), 91–106.

7   Zöe Franklin, 'William Babel's [*sic*] *Concertos in Seven Parts*, *The Consort*, 63 (2007), 62–73.

comprehensively reviewed by Peter Holman and Richard Maunder, these authors giving insight not only into orchestration but also into performance practice.[8] Their work will be incorporated and augmented in my discussion of the structure of the concerti.

As I have noted, the small flute concerti are a uniquely English contribution to the repertoire of the recorder, but no organological study of small recorders exists, nor has the harmonic development of most of the concerti been described; many performances of the pieces are documented in playbills and concert notices of the early eighteenth century.[9] The use of transposed recorder parts so that the player read as if playing an alto recorder in f' has been noted since the eighteenth century, but the selection of the keys in which the concerti are written has not been discussed in relation to the particular characteristics of fifth and sixth flutes. The technical demands of the small flute concerti have not been assessed in relation to the abilities of professional or amateur players, nor have the reasons for the use of small recorders (as opposed to altos) for 'interval music' in the theatres been examined. It is not known, at present, why English composers chose fifth and sixth flutes in preference to altos or sopraninos, and a comparison of the particular use of various types of recorder in England as compared with Continental Europe has not hitherto been published in the literature.

It is the purpose of this monograph to address these questions, examining the musical life of early eighteenth-century London, the recorders themselves and the concerti. Beyond the purely factual, the particular role of the small flute concerti and their small recorders will be contextualised within both English and European musical culture of the early eighteenth century.

1.3. Theatres, concert halls, and performance

Early eighteenth-century London was ranked as one of the musical capitals of the world: public concerts had been established by John Banister in 1672 and professional public performances were given in theatres, concert rooms, taverns, the halls of livery companies and in pleasure gardens.
[10] For each documented performance, there must have been a plethora of other performances, professional and amateur, public and private. In the early eighteenth century, London numbered amongst its citizens many native musicians, but also a great number of foreign composers, players and singers: two composers of small flute concerti — Charles Dieupart and Guiseppe Sammartini — were immigrants from France and Italy respectively. Records exist of the small flute concerti being performed in theatres and concert rooms between the years of 1717 and 1734.

8 Peter Holman and Richard Maunder, 'The Accompaniment of Concertos in 18th-Century England', *Early Music*, 28/4 (2000), 37–50; Richard Maunder, *The Scoring of Baroque Concertos* (Woodbridge: The Boydell Press, 2004).

9 *The London Stage 1660–1800. A Calendar of Plays, Entertainments, and Afterpieces, Together with Casts, Box-receipts and Contemporary Comment Compiled from the Playbills, Newspapers and Theatrical Diaries of the Period*, 5 parts, (Carbondale: Southern Illinois University Press, 1960–1968); Part 1: 1660–1700, ed. by William Van Lennep, (1960); Part 2: 1700–1729, ed. by Emmett L. Avery, (1960); Part 3, ed. by Arthur H. Scrouton, (1968).

10 Nicholas Temperley, et.al.,'London (i)', *Grove Music Online. Oxford Music Online*, Oxford University Press, accessed 19 November 2015. http://www.oxfordmusiconline.com/subscriber/article/grove/music/16904pg5.

Many performances of small flute concerti were given as 'interval music' in the London theatres, and documentation exists of performances also being given in concert rooms.[11] The suitability of the concerti for performance in the known venues requires further discussion, as does the possibility of amateur performance. A brief survey of the venues available for the citizens of London to hear concerted music will form a background to small flute concerto performances between the years 1717 and 1734.

In 1663 King Charles II (reigned 1660–85) issued licences for only two theatres to perform plays spoken in the English language, a decree which influenced London theatres before the introduction of the Licensing Act of 1737 which continued similar restrictions and was finally effectively withdrawn in 1843, although the Lord Chamberlain continued to exercise censorship until 1968. The Theatre Royal in Drury Lane was established in 1663, and a new building (designed by Sir Christopher Wren) was opened in 1674. The Lincoln's Inn Fields Theatre was initially a tennis court but opened as a theatre *c.*1661 and from 1695 was licensed to perform plays in English under the management of Thomas Betterton. John Rich became its manager in 1714 before establishing the Theatre Royal, Covent Garden in 1732, at which time the licence for English plays was transferred to Covent Garden. The Lincoln's Inn Fields theatre finally closed in 1746.

Opera (being sung and in the Italian tongue) was not subjected to the Licensing Act and could be performed at 'unlicensed' venues, as could musical entertainments.[12] The Queen's Theatre in the Haymarket was built by Sir John Vanburgh (*c.*1664–1726) in 1705, becoming the King's Theatre after the accession of George I in 1714 and was much used by Handel: on the opposite side of the Haymarket, the Little Theatre opened in 1721. However, the majority of Londoners took little interest in Italian opera, preferring the mixed repertoire on offer at Drury Lane and Covent Garden.[13] The season ran from September to May, but the Little Theatre in the Haymarket was only open in the summer months when the major theatres were closed 'out of season'. The first Goodman's Fields Theatre in the less-salubrious area of south Whitechapel opened in 1727, but was replaced by a new building in the same street in 1732: it closed after the introduction of the rigorous Licensing Act of 1737 but re-opened in 1740. It is beyond the scope of this brief review to list all the theatres in London and the provinces, but suffice it to note that John Baston performed at Penkethman's Theatre in Richmond in 1723.

1.4. Financial and social considerations

It is appropriate to consider the cost of attendance at concerts and theatres in relation to income when considering the social status of patrons at artistic events. In the early eighteenth century, a labourer earned around £20 *per annum*, a journeyman (a trained craftsman) could earn around £39, an artisan craftsman £55, and a skilled cabinet maker as much as £90. These figures equate to 8s., 15s., £1, and £4 14s. per week respectively.[14] Living costs remained fairly constant until inflation set in late in the eighteenth century, when pay rises failed to keep up with the cost of living. A rank-and-file orchestral player in the first quarter of the eighteenth century could expect to receive £40 for a forty-week season (close to the pay of a journeyman in the period), but many players augmented their income by teaching. Players in theatre orchestras who gave performances on stage for interval music would be paid upwards of 3s. 4d. extra, and the distinguished recorder player James Paisible, for example, was

---

11   Roger Fiske, *English Theatre Music in the Eighteenth Century* (Oxford: 2nd. edn, Oxford University Press, 1986), p.259.

12   The licence to perform English dramas was issued to the manager rather than to the theatre.

13   Roger Fiske in H.Diack Johnstone and Roger Fiske, (eds.), *The Blackwell History of Music in Britain: the Eighteenth Century* (Oxford: Basil Blackwell, 1990), p.16.

14   Prior to decimalisation in 1971, in English currency £1 = 20 shillings (s), 1 shilling = 12 pence (d); Figures averaged from Jerry White, *London in the Eighteenth Century* (London: Vintage Books, 2013), p.234.

paid 5s. per day with an extra guinea (£1 1s.) by the management at Drury Lane when he performed on stage.[15]

Eighteenth-century theatre auditoria were divided into boxes (either in front of the stage or at the sides), the pit, which was separated from the stage by the orchestra, and one or two galleries. There was a financially-inevitable social division in terms of the occupancy of the various seats, although there was less social distinction than often thought. People from all walks of life from the aristocracy through the middle classes to apprentices and even servants attended theatres. Front boxes were usually filled by ladies and the aristocracy, whereas younger men (and prostitutes touting for trade!) occupied the pit, and the lower echelons of society sat in the upper or lower gallery. Ticket prices in the early eighteenth century were particularly high in the world of Italian opera at the Queen's/King's Theatre: in 1705, admission to a box would have cost 10s. 6d., whereas seats in the pit or galleries could be procured for 5s. For admission to other theatres, patrons would usually pay around 5s. for a box, 3s. for a seat in the pit, 2s. and 1s. for the lower and upper galleries respectively. Concerts were somewhat cheaper. Jerry White comments that 'A shilling was a manageable sum for an artisan and an occasional treat for a journeyman'.[16]

1.5. Performance venues

An evening at the theatre

In contrast to twenty-first century evenings at the theatre at which one play is perfomed, early eighteenth-centuries audiences often enjoyed a much longer evening with various entertainments before, during, and after the main attraction of the evening's programme. Before the play began, there would be three pieces of music performed by the orchestra (known as the first, second and third music, and lasting for about half an hour) followed by the principal play, which was sometimes introduced by an actor speaking a Prologue. The following poem, taken from *The Green Room* of 1742, describes the opening music:

> In former times no orchestra was known
> But thrice before the play, a horn was blown…
> But since the Aera of the Restoration
> The Playhouses got politer with the Nation.
> Drums, Kettle-Drums, and Trumpets, Hautboys,
> Flutes, Violoncellos, Violins, and Lutes,
> Concerts, Concertos, Overtures and Airs,
> Are all now us'd to introduce the Players.[17]

The main play could contain one or more *entr'acte* entertainments, and may have been concluded by an Epilogue preceding the afterpiece. This shorter and lighter portion of the evening's entertainment may have been short play (often of a 'lighter' character such as a farce), a pantomime, or even a one-act opera.[18] The most popular *entr'acte* was dancing, followed by singing but instrumental music appears to have been less popular: whether the popularity of dance can shed any light on the prevailing taste of differing social classes is impossible to determine. It is as 'interval music' that the small flute concerti assumed particular prominence, and these performances will be further discussed in Chapter 4.

---

15   *The London Stage, 1660–1800, Part 2*, p.cxxxvi.
16   Rosamond McGuinness and H. Diack Johnstone 'Concert Life in England I' in *The Blackwell History of Music in Britain: the Eighteenth Century*, p.41; White, *London in the Eighteenth Century*, p.307.
17   *The London Stage, 1660–1800…Part 2, 1700–1729*, p.cxxxvi.
18   Roger Fiske, *English Theatre Music in the Eighteenth Century*, p.259.

Concert rooms, Pleasure Gardens, and taverns

The introduction of public concerts in London allowed entrepreneurs and impresarios to open concert rooms, the most notable of which were Hickford's Rooms in Soho and York Buildings in Villiers Street off The Strand. The premises at York Buildings opened in *c.*1680; John Baston performed there at least in 1720 and again in 1728 but the premises closed in 1732. Maunder notes – in relation to his contention that concerti were performed one-to-a-part – that the size of the performing space (15'9" deep, 17' in diameter) is hardly a large enough space for more than single strings, soloist(s) and a harpsichord.[19] There is no record of small flute concerti being performed at the house of the 'musical small coals man' Thomas Britton of Clerkenwell (1644–1714) but, amongst his effects, were found concerti 'by the young Mr. Babel', which could have included the small flute concerti.[20] The dancing master Thomas Hickford established concerts in his rooms between Panton Street and Brewer Street (Soho) in 1697, moving to more spacious premises in Brewer Street in 1738. Mozart and his sister Nannerl performed in the rooms in 1765, and, of relevance to the present study, John Baston performed at Hickford's in 1720 and Jack Kytch played one of Babell's concerti there in 1729.[21]

In the later years of the eighteenth century, the Pleasure Gardens became important venues for both musical entertainment and social integration, although the latter was sometimes of a morally dubious nature. There is little evidence of small flute concerti being performed in the Pleasure Gardens, perhaps because the gardens became more popular in the latter years of the eighteenth century when the era of small flute concerti had passed its zenith. However, two concerti for the little flute were performed at Marylebone Gardens on 12 July 1738, but neither composer nor performer were named in the newspaper advertisement.[22]

Although there is only one documented performance of small flute concerti in London's inns and taverns, it is appropriate to note their importance as venues for music-making: the Crown and Anchor in Arundel Street, the Devil's Tavern at Temple Bar and the Mitre at Greenwich may be taken as examples. Performances of music were given in the halls of the City of London livery companies, and the name of John Baston is first noted in 1709, when he performed a concerto grosso with his violinist brother, Thomas (*fl*1708–27) at Stationers' Hall.[23] The Bastons also gave benefit concerts at the Coach-Makers' Hall (1711) and the Stationers' Hall (1712), but the music played is not listed. It should be recalled that Thomas was a violinist and John a 'cellist as well as a recorder player, so they may have performed string music.

1.6. Professionals, amateurs, and gender.

Histories of music tend – perhaps inevitably – to focus on professional public performance in capital cities, but it should be recalled that much (if not most) music was played by amateurs for their own satisfaction as well as for public performance. In England, there was an abundance of musical activity in the major towns and cities, particularly in such places as Bath, Newcastle, Norwich, Oxford, and the cathedral cities. Outside England, both Dublin and Edinburgh were important musical centres.

---

19   Maunder, *The Scoring of Baroque Concertos*, p.112; (*c.*5m x 5.2m)

20   John Hawkins, *A General History of the Science and Practice of Music* (London: T. Payne & Son, 1776), note, p.608; Thomas Britton was a small coals merchant who promoted concerts in a small room at his house in Clerkenwell between 1678 and 1714. Despite an unattractive venue, his concerts attracted notable musicians (including Handel) and members of 'society'.

21   Robert Elkin, *The Old Concert Rooms of London* (London: Edward Arnold, 1955), pp.42–49.

22   *London Daily Post and General Advertiser*, 10 July 1738.

23   *Daily Courant*, 24 August 1709.

Much of the provincial musical activity was led by amateurs (often with professional stiffening) but there is no record of the small flute concerti being performed either outside of London or in the domestic salon.[24] David Lasocki discussed the activities of the amateur recorder players Claver Morris and Dudley Ryder in an article in *American Recorder* in 1999, but there is apparently no evidence for their use of small recorders.[25] However, the Mackworth Collection, established by the Neathe (South Wales) industrialist Sir Herbert Mackworth (1737–91) and now in the library of the University of Wales, Cardiff, contains an incomplete set of parts for the Woodcock concerti.[26] This may suggest an amateur domestic use, especially considering that Woodcock's technical demands could be met by a skilled amateur player. However, as Fiona Smith writes 'It must be borne in mind that far more sets [of playing parts] have been lost than have survived, and the gaps in the surviving evidence are therefore considerable'.[27] Homes, theatres, concert halls and individual musicians would almost certainly have lost or discarded music they no longer required, and it is most unlikely that the number of copies of the concerti sold by the leading publishers of recorder music, Walsh and Hare, will ever be known. No firm conclusions may be drawn regarding the amateur performance of small flute concerti – or whether they may have been played by both men and women. In the early eighteenth century, most female musicians confined their attention to keyboard instruments: the violin, the 'cello and (particularly) wind instruments were played by men. There was a certain opposition to women playing wind instruments, for the embouchure gave rise to facial distortion and the oboe and recorder had phallic implications. John Essex, in his *The Young Ladies Conduct* of 1722 wrote:

> The *Harpsichord, Spinnet, Lute* and *Base Violin*, are Instruments most agreeable to the Ladies: there are some others that really are unbecoming to the Fair Sex; as the *Flute, Violin* and *Hautboy*; the last of which is too Manlike and would look indecent in a Woman's Mouth; and the Flute is very improper, as taking away too much of the Juices, which are otherwise more necessarily employ'd, to promote the Appetite, and assist Digestion.[28]

However, there is some evidence that women did play the recorder. In 1711, the *Tatler* quoted a letter from a Belinda to a Mr Isaac Bickerstaff 'I could with infinite Pleasure rove about the Wilderness, in our Garden, and charm the Rival Nightingales with the Musick of my Flute'.[29] An obituary published in the *Grub Street Journal* in 1733 noted the passing of 'Monsieur de Moinor, very famous for teaching young gentlemen and ladies on the flute, and other instruments'.[30]

The earliest reference to a performance on small flutes is to be found in an announcement in the *Spectator* of 21 November 1715 at a benefit concert for a Mr. Cook which included 'Octave Flutes' but the majority of documented performances of small flute concerti took place in the theatres,

---

24   Stanley Sadie, 'Concert Life in Eighteenth-Century England', *Proceedings of the Royal Musical Association* 85 (1958-59), 17.

25   David Lasocki, 'Amateur Recorder playing in Renaissance and Baroque England', *American Recorder*, 40/1 (1999), 15–18.

26   Shelfmark 3.56.

27   Fiona Smith, 'Original Performing Material for Concerted Music in England, *c.*1660–1800', PhD diss., University of Leeds (2014), p.332.

28   John Essex, *The Young Ladies Conduct: or, Rules for Education*, (London: 1722), pp.84–5.

29   *Tatler*, 14–17 April 2011: Fiona Smith has suggested that the letter may not be from 'Belinda' but written by a member of the editorial staff. Dr Smith notes that the letter contains material with erotic connotations with regard to the recorder (flute) and the nightingale. Perhaps Belinda was behaving badly – an inference which an eighteenth-century reader would probably have made!

30   *Grub Street Journal*, 6 September 1733.

notably Lincoln's Inn Fields and Drury Lane, the most frequent performer being Baston.[31] The concerti were inserted into the evening's programme as 'interval music' and, as we have seen, an evening at the theatre usually contained several episodes. Theatre orchestras usually numbered around twenty players, and it seems likely that the concerto soloist would perform on the stage although no evidence for this practice is forthcoming: the orchestra would have remained seated in the pit.

The small flute concerti were performed as interval or *entr'acte* music, and were usually announced – together with dancing and vocal music – in the playbills and newspaper advertisements as forming an integral part of the evening's entertainment. The music to be performed was often cited in advertising material, and a similar custom pertained to dance and singing. Two examples shall suffice. On 6 November 1716 at Lincoln's Inn Fields Theatre *The City Wives Confederacy* was accompanied by dancing '*French Peasant* by Moreau and Mrs Cross. *Dutch Skipper* by Salle and Mlle Salle' and on 20 April 1721 the audience at *The Island Princess* heard 'The *Enthusiastic Song* and Dialogues by Le Garde and Pack'.[32] Theatre performances of the small flute concerti will be discussed further in Chapter 4. By the late 1720's fewer performances of the concerti were advertised, and John Baston's final performance appears to have been at Drury Lane in 1733: one of Woodcock's concerti was given at Goodman's Fields Theatre in 1734. However, the concerti continued to appear in publisher's catalogues until 1776, by which time their genre and style was long out-moded.

1.7. Discussion

Forming an English contribution to the repertoire of the recorder, the small flute concerti have not – with a few exceptions – been subjected to a critical analysis, particularly in connection with selected keys, and harmonic structure. Aspects of performance practice regarding the audibility of the recorder in a string ensemble and the possible use of the concerti by amateur players have not been addressed. A brief comparison of the Continental use of fifth and sixth flutes indicates that continental composers nearly always scored their recorder concerti for the alto, and no concerti for fifth or sixth flutes from continental Europe have come to light in the course of my study: this observation furthers my hypothesis that the concerti are a product of an English musical culture.

It is the purpose of the present volume to present a comprehensive and critical review of the small flute concerto in England in the early eighteenth century. Chapter 2 will be devoted to an organological discussion centred on small recorders, and the third chapter will consider the concerti in detail, giving salient biographical details of the composers before a critical discussion of each of the extant concerti in relation to keys, harmonic structure, and orchestration. A final chapter will be devoted to matters of performance and a discussion of the unique position of the small flute concerti within the global recorder repertoire.

---

31   *Spectator*, 21 November 1715; 'a consort for the benefit of Mr Cook with Hautboys, German Flute, Kettledrums, Trumpets, Octave Flutes, Violins, and Singing by several masters' was given at the Barbers' and Surgeons' Hall in Mugwell Street. The repertoire is not known.

32   *The London Stage* 2, pp.421, 625.

Chapter 2

The recorder

2.1. Abstract of the chapter

This chapter outlines the organology of the Baroque recorder and its suitability for playing in various keys. Small recorders ('flutes') are discussed with particular reference to their usage in England, and a table of surviving Baroque octave recorders of English manufacture is included (further details of the instruments are given in Appendix 1). The chapter concludes with a brief discussion on pedagogy and a comparison with the use of small recorders in England and on the European mainland.

2.2. The Baroque recorder

Until the late seventeenth century, the recorder existed in what is now known as the 'Renaissance style' of the instrument. It had a substantially cylindrical bore and large tone-holes, giving a strong sound rich in the fundamental but lacking in the higher harmonics. Various types of the instrument existed, with different bore profiles: the most common had a compass of an octave and a sixth, but the later *handfluyt* had a compass of two octaves and a second, as did the 'transitional' recorders, exemplified by those of Hieronimus Franciscus Kynseker of Nuremburg (*fl*1673–86).

By the late seventeenth century the true Baroque recorder had come into being. There are no contemporaneous manufacturers' announcements of the new instrument, but it is generally considered that the re-modelling of the recorder was the work of the Hotteterre dynasty in La Couture-Boussey, France.[33] The largely cylindrical wide bore of the renaissance recorder had become a narrow inverted cone, with continued contraction through the length of the foot-joint. A choke was sometimes applied around the level of the lowest tone-hole and both this and the continuing contraction of the bore facilitated the fingering of the highest notes, using the third register for the upper notes of the second octave and the fourth register for the third octave. 'Chambers' were reamed into the bore for the purposes of tuning and improving tone quality, thus producing slight deviation from the smooth contracting inverted cone.

The tone-holes were smaller than those on Renaissance recorders and sometimes undercut; undercutting effectively widens the bore when the hole is closed by the player's finger and so affects tuning. The complex bore profile with its chambering could no longer be reamed in one piece of wood and, as a consequence, the recorder became multi-jointed. The basic bore could be drilled, and then adjusted with reamers passed from the end of the tube. The characteristic bulges and ornamental turnery applied at the joints was functional (to strengthen the joints) as well as aesthetic, and ivory mounts were applied to many recorders.

Figure 1. Late eighteenth-century Baroque recorder (voice flute), stamped 'METZLER/LONDON/105 WARDOUR ST'.[34]

---

33   Hunt, *The Recorder and its Music*, pp. 37–8.

34   Author's collection.

The result was a recorder with a more penetrating reedy sound suited to both chamber and orchestral playing; the instrument had a standard compass of two octaves and a second (f'–g''' on an alto in f'), although higher notes could be obtained on a fine instrument by an expert player. The seventh-finger note was commonly f', as illustrated by surviving instruments, music and tutors (French, English and German) and the F recorder remained the standard alto (treble) recorder throughout the late seventeenth and eighteenth centuries.

The French Baroque recorder appears to have arrived in England in September 1673, when four oboists/recorder players accompanied the composer Robert Cambert on a cross-channel voyage from France.[35] The men (Jacques Paisible, Maxent De Bremes, Pierre Guitot and [?Jean] Boutet) were players of the newly-developed Baroque oboe and recorder and it is likely that all the recorders used in England before this time were of the Renaissance type.[36] In France, the recorder was known as *la flûte douce* or *la flûte à bec* and it is probable that either or both of these terms were contracted in English usage to 'flute'; in late seventeenth- and early eighteenth-century England the word 'flute' normally implied the recorder.[37]

Fingering on the Baroque recorder and suitability for particular keys

There are certain acoustical features relating to woodwind instruments in general and to the recorder in particular which determine their suitability for playing music in particular keys. This is especially significant in the case of the recorder as the instrument was not fitted with keys to facilitate chromatic semitones but recorders are available in several pitches, each with different tonal characteristics.[38] The small flute concerti were conceived for the fifth and sixth flutes, and the following discussion will serve to indicate the reasons for the choice of sharp keys for these instruments.

As a general principle, notes are produced on a woodwind instrument by the shortening hole system, whereby the raising of successive fingers produces a natural scale: in organological discussion this scale is customarily described as beginning on the sixth-finger note, but many instruments (including recorders) have a downward extension to allow the seventh finger to be utilised to extend the downward range of the instrument by a tone. The natural scale sounded on an instrument with G as its sixth-finger note — such as an alto recorder — is G, A, B, C, D, E, F-sharp: it would be expected that to obtain the chromatic semitones of B-flat, C-sharp, E-flat and F, fork- or cross-fingerings would have to be employed.[39] The bore of the recorder, however, dictates that the fourth note of the scale (B-natural on an alto recorder) is sounded as a flattened version of the third-finger note and fingered 0123–56–, whereas the true fourth-finger note has to be flattened to produce B-flat (01234–67). When holes below the sounding hole are closed, the pitch is lowered but also the tone becomes more veiled. It is apparent that playing in a key which requires many fork- or cross-fingerings is not

35   David Lasocki, 'Professional Recorder Playing in England 1500–1740: Part 2', *Early Music*, 10/2 (1982), 182–191.

36   Renaissance recorders were still known in England in the 1690s: a *vanitas* painting dated 1696 (Still Life with a Volume of Withers "Emblemes") by Edward Collier (active 1662–1702) shows the upper part of a Renaissance recorder with a metal sleeve on the mouthpiece and also bowed and plucked stringed instruments (oil on canvas, Tate Britain N05916).

37   Very few English recorders survive from this period, but an ivory alto by the late seventeenth-century English maker Goddard has recently been acquired by the Bate Collection, University of Oxford (January 2017).

38   The key for the lowest note on the basset recorder is not a chromatic key: it serves to bring the seventh tone-hole within the reach of the player's little finger.

39   Adam Carse, *Musical Wind Instruments* (New York: 1939, repr. Da Capo Press, 1956), p.27; it is customary to describe recorders in terms of their seventh-finger note, *i.e.* an alto recorder with a seventh-finger note of f' is described as a recorder in F.

only more difficult for the player but will also produce a more muted effect.[40] In practical terms, the notes affected by fork-fingerings in flat keys on the alto recorder are B-flat, E-flat and A-flat and D-flat, whereas the keys of C and G require no fork-fingerings. It follows that the instrument will sound brighter in C and G than in flat keys: this is, however, an acoustic effect and not influenced by the 'character' of the keys in terms of equal-tempered tuning. The notes of #IV and bVII involve fingerings which require closing of tone holes above and below the 'note-hole' (although they are not true fork-fingerings) and the sixth finger is required in the case of IV to bring the note into tune (0123–56–).[41] In the case of bVII, the first hole is vented and the thumb-hole closed (0–2– – – – –). The problem of finding an adequate fingering for #I"/bII" (f-sharp"') — the only chromatic note unobtainable on the Baroque recorder — was not satisfactorily resolved until the advent of the bell key in the twentieth century. Curiously, the equivalent note on the sixth flute (d-sharp"') is required in the opening movement of Robert Woodcock's first concerto in E major.

On the soprano recorder (fifth flute in C) the keys avoiding multiple fork-fingerings are G, D and A: the key of C major requires a fork-fingering for F-natural, but only two fork-fingerings are required in the more remote key of E major. The preferred keys for the alto are C, G and D and, for the soprano, G, D and A: this preference for the sharp keys (particularly for the soprano) comes further into focus when considering the sixth flute or voice flute, both being built in D. In contrast, the fourth flute in B-flat is more suited to flat keys, as is the B-flat clarinet.

Examination of the fingering for the sixth flute in D (lowest note notated d') reveals that fork-fingerings are required for G, B-flat and C natural in the first octave, together with E-flat, G, B-flat, C and D in the second. Again, this instrument is more suited to playing in the sharp keys of A, E and D, which avoid most fork-fingerings. A further concern with the sixth flute arises in respect to its notation: recorder music in the twentieth and twenty-first centuries is not transposed (except for the octave) and players use both F and C fingerings as a matter of course. To play a sixth flute with a D fingering is confusing and it is easier to transpose down a tone and use C fingering or up a third and use F fingering. In the eighteenth century, however, music for both sixth and fifth flutes was transposed a sixth or fifth lower so that the player read as if he were playing an alto recorder. Not only did the player have to cope with learning only one fingering, but also — in the case of the sixth flute — the use of alto fingering simplified playing by removing the forks required for the commonly-used notes of G and C-natural. Of the seventeen concerti, sixteen are in sharp keys.

Applying these arguments, it is apparent why composers selected sharp keys for fifth and sixth flute concerti.[42] Problems of audibility may be encountered using alto recorders in concerti, as the instrument is relatively soft and plays at approximately the same pitch as an accompanying string ensemble, but with the use of octave recorders, this problem is minimised.

2.3. The small recorders

The small flute concerti were composed for small Baroque-style recorders which include the fourth, fifth, sixth and octave flutes, named in relation to their pitch above the alto in f'; in the eighteenth century, these instruments were called 'little' or 'small' flutes. The sixth flute is pitched a sixth above the alto, and the fifth flute (soprano or descant) a fifth above; the term 'fourth flute' in the present

---

40   One of the functions of keys on a woodwind instrument is to allow the tone holes to be placed in their acoustically correct position and so avoid the necessity for fork- or cross-fingering.

41   Roman numerals are employed to indicate tone-holes in acoustical discussion: for example, the note V on a recorder implies the note sounded when the thumb-hole and first three finger-holes are closed. Arabic numerals are employed to denote fingering.

42   Nine are in D, three in A, one in E: one each are in the keys of E minor, B minor, and A minor, and only one concerto is written in the flat key of F.

context applies to the recorder in b-flat', but may also be applied to the tenor in c', a fourth below the alto. The modern term for the true octave recorder (an octave above the alto) is 'sopranino', but the word was not utilised in the eighteenth century, the instrument falling within the category of 'small' or 'little' flute. It is for the fifth and particularly the sixth flutes that the English small flute concerti were composed, the fourth flute being rarely used, and never as a concerto instrument. Fifth flutes were occasionally used orchestrally, but sixth flutes in were only employed in England as concerto instruments.[43] The sopranino often featured as an obbligato instrument, particularly in a 'bird imitation' role, and continued to do so until the latter half of the eighteenth century, but it was not used in concerti by English composers.[44] Curiously, only one sopranino of English origin appears to have survived (see Table 1).

In contrast, the fifth flute was more commonly required by composers in mainland Europe, but no concerti for the instrument by these composers are extant. The sixth flute was very occasionally used in obbligato passages by Bach and Telemann, but, again, there are no concerti. A review of Nicholas Lander's website 'The Recorder Homepage' which contains listings of historical recorders revealed only three sixth flutes from mainland Europe: I have listed eleven surviving English examples of small flutes below, but only two are sixth flutes (Table 1). [45] Vivaldi's three concerti for the sopranino (RV 442, 443, and 444) are well-known works assigned to this smallest member of the Baroque recorder family.

As I have noted, the most commonly encountered recorder in the late-seventeenth and eighteenth centuries is the alto (treble) in f' and the literature contains publications which discuss the small proportion of extant small recorders compared with altos. Anthony Baines, writing in the first volume of the *Galpin Society Journal*, discussed James Talbot's manuscript in the library of Christ Church College, Oxford, dating from c.1685–c.1701.[46] Talbot lists a flageolet, a tabor-pipe and a fife. He gives the pitch of recorders including 8th, 5th and 3rd flutes as well as larger recorders including consort and voice flutes, tenor, bass and great bass recorders.[47] This document represents the earliest indication of the existence of octave flutes in England at the end of the seventeenth century.

Eric Halfpenny's study of the English baroque treble recorder is confined, as the title suggests, to the treble (alto) recorder. Halfpenny lists forty-three recorders found in English collections. Of these, nineteen are altos but he notes that only four are described as 'super trebles', including 6th, 5th and 4th flutes. Unfortunately, the pitch of seven of the forty-three instruments could not be identified.[48] From this study, it is apparent that the smaller recorders were considerably less common than altos or the larger recorders.

David Lasocki's meticulously researched 'Lessons from Inventories and Sales of Flutes and Recorders, 1650–1800' discusses terminology in relation to the words 'flute' and 'recorder', and the various sizes of flutes and recorders encountered in the survey.[49] Lasocki gives a concluding table including makers, the numbers of instruments they advertised and the number of surviving specimens. The advertisements listed in the table do not always specify the type of recorder, but a review of the

43   Handel gave small parts to fifth flutes in his *Water Music* of 1717 and in his opera *Alcina* of 1737.

44   Douglas MacMillan, 'The Sopranino Recorder in England, 1750 – 1800', *A Handbook for Studies in 18th.-Century Music*, 22 (2018), 19 – 25.

45   N.S.Lander, 'Instruments', The Recorder Home Page (1996–2016), www.recorderhomepage.net/instruments/, (accessed 5 March 2018).

46   Anthony Baines, 'James Talbot's Manuscript', *Galpin Society Journal*, 1 (1948), 9–26.

47   The consort flute is the alto in f', the voice flute is pitched in d' and the tenor in c' Basses are in f or c.

48   Eric Halfpenny, 'The English Baroque Treble Recorder', *Galpin Society Journal*, 9 (1956), 82–90.

49   David Lasocki, 'Lessons from inventories and sales of flutes and recorders', www.instantharmony.net. Music/lessons-from-the-inventories.pdf./(accessed 11–17 March 2014).

surviving 283 instruments reveals an interesting pattern in relation to octave recorders. Out of the 283, only 35 are small recorders as against 161 altos and 68 voice flutes, tenors and basses. Nineteen miscellaneous instruments (including double recorders and cane recorders) make up the total. Although the listings in this paper are derived from both European and American sources, the tiny proportion of small recorders in relation to larger ones is of considerable interest. Only five English makers are listed, and again the proportion of small recorders is low in proportion to altos and larger instruments. Taken together, the publications of Halfpenny and Lasocki indicate that small recorders are rare in comparison with altos, both in the eighteenth century and those surviving in present-day instrument collections. It is therefore hardly surprising that the surviving repertoire for these instruments is small, a matter which increases the significance of the English small flute concerti.

2.4. Octave recorders in England

The earliest of the major English recorder makers, Peter Jaillard Bressan and Thomas Stanesby, sr., only began work in 1688 and 1691 respectively, although a few instruments by the French Hotteterre dynasty survive in Paris.[50] The English recorder repertoire of the period is almost all written for the alto recorder, although some parts would require the lower range of the voice flute or tenor if the music were not transposed into a higher key. There is no trace of octave recorders until the account given in James Talbot's manuscript.[51] I have undertaken an extensive review of the checklists available on the internet, which include not only collection catalogues but also two major electronic databases and have only discovered eleven octave recorders of English manufacture made by five makers.[52] These are listed in Table 1 and organological data are given Appendix 1. As I have noted above, a similar situation arises regarding instruments made in mainland Europe although fifth flutes and sopraninos were relatively common. The English makers of the identified small recorders are Peter Jaillard Bressan (1688–1730), Thomas Stanesby, sr. (1691–1733/4), Thomas Stanesby, jr. (1713–54), Benjamin Hallett (1736–53), John Just Schuchart (1731–53) and John Mason (*fl a*1754–*p*1756): the table on the following page indicates the proportion of all the surviving recorders by these makers.[53] Appendix 1 summarises the known organological data on each of these instruments.

	8th flute	6th flute	5th flute	4th flute	alto	tenor[54]	basset
Bressan				1	37	30	10
Stanesby sr.		1			10	2	1
Stanesby jr.		1	2	1	12	6	
Hallett	1		1	1			
Schuchart			1		7		
Mason			1				

Table 1. Octave Recorders by English Makers

50   *The New Langwill Index*, ed. by William Waterhouse (London: Tony Bingham, 1993), p.182.

51   Baines, 'James Talbot's Manuscript'.

52   N.S.Lander, 'Instruments', The Recorder Home Page (1996–2016), www.recorderhomepage.net/instruments/, (accessed 17 July 2017); Musical Instrument Museums Online, www.mimo-international.com (accessed 17 July 2017): these list a total of 1868 recorders of all nationalities (July 2017).

53   The dates given indicate the years of activity as given in *The New Langwill Index*.

54   Includes voice flutes and tenors.

Unfortunately the data available on five of the octave recorders is minimal, as three are held in private collections, and in one case the collection checklist contains only limited information; a further instrument is incomplete.

Figure 2. Fourth flute by Bressan[55]

The instrument collection left by Samuel Hellier at his death in 1784 contained 'Two Octave Flutes, one German, one Comn. form by Gedney' as well as a common flute, a fife and a bird flageolet.[56] There is also some evidence that small recorders were being made up to the turn of the eighteenth and nineteenth centuries in that the catalogues of George Astor and George Goulding (*c.*1799 and *c.*1803 respectively) advertise English Concert Flutes (recorders) and also '2nd., 3rd., 4th., 5th., 6th. and Octave' versions.[57] In the catalogue, these instruments are clearly distinguished from transverse 'German' flutes. None of these instruments survive and there does not appear to be an assigned repertoire for alto recorders as late as 1800, although composers occasionally called for small recorders until 1793.

2.5. Pedagogy

Eighteenth-century recorder methods were published, without exception, for the alto recorder: it was not until William Tansur's universal tutor *A New Musical Grammar* of 1746 that any method referred to small recorders, but, by the time of its publication the recorder was in decline, and no small flute concerti had been published for seventeen years. Tans'ur wrote that 'Of *Flutes* there are many sorts, as a *Consort-Flute*; a *Third-Flute*; a *Fifth*, a *Sixth*, and *Octave-Flute*, yet all may be play'd by the foregoing rules'.[58] It is reasonable to assume that 'play'd by the foregoing rules' implies that all the instruments are played using alto fingering. It can only be assumed that players – particularly professionals – would have adapted to the transposition as a matter of course

---

55   With permission of the Bate Collection, Faculty of Music, University of Oxford, 0109: author's photograph.

56   Samuel Hellier, 'A Catalogue of Musicall Instruments', *Galpin Society Journal*, 18 (1965), 5–6; Caleb Gedney worked between 1754 and 1769.

57   David Lasocki, 'New Light on Eighteenth-Century English Woodwind Makers', *Galpin Society Journal*, 63 (2010), 73–142.

58   William Tans'ur, *A New Musical Grammar: or, the Harmonical Spectator...* (for the author, 1746), p.83.

2.6. Discussion

The principal organological question regarding the English small flute concerti is 'why the sixth flute?' Of the seventeen concerti and the anonymous suite, one or two sixth flutes are required in fifteen (there are four pieces for two sixth flutes) whereas fifth flutes are only required in three concerti. Admittedly, all the sixth flute pieces lie in sharp keys, so the question arises *post hoc* or *propter hoc*: did the composers choose sharp keys and sixth flutes because they were readily available, or did the makers respond to composers' demands? A comparison with continental European use strongly suggests that sixth flutes were essentially an English phenomenon, despite most Baroque recorders (from sopranino to basset) being built in F or C. Further light may be shed on the English use of D recorders if one examines the extant voice flutes ('tenors' in d'): of thirty-eight such instruments in Lander's list of historic recorders, eighteen are of English origin, Bressan being the most significant maker. It seems that recorders in D (sixth flutes and voice flutes) were favoured in England, but, at present, I am unable to find a reason for this. The voice flute itself remains something of an enigma, for, despite the survival of many instruments, little assigned repertoire exists: the common assumption is that players used the voice flute to play transverse flute music (lowest note d') but I have yet to find contemporary evidence for this practice.

The more common fifth flute is only required in three concerti: more of these instruments survive than sopraninos, sixth and fourth flutes but the repertoire (in either English or continental usage) remains small. Further research may reveal a reason for the English propensity to build recorders in D, either voice flutes or sixth flutes: at least, it is easy to explain the use of sixth flutes for concerti composed in sharp keys.

Chapter 3

The small flute concerti

3.1. Abstract of the chapter

Following a general introduction outlining the small flute concerti, the structure, orchestration, and harmonic development of the concerti are discussed. The seventeen concerti by the composers William Babell, John Baston, Robert Woodcock, Charles Dieupart, and Giuseppe Sammartini are critically and comparatively discussed in respect of their harmony and orchestration, together with an anonymous suite for sixth flute. Brief biographies of the composers are given.

3.2. Introduction

By the early eighteenth century, the term 'concerto' was generally applied to a musical composition contrasting an instrument (or group of instruments) with an accompanying instrumental ensemble. In the case of the English small flute (recorder) concerti, the solo instrument was a fifth or sixth flute (or two sixth flutes), contrasted with a string ensemble of variable composition and an accompanying keyboard instrument.[59] The seventeen extant small flute concerti were composed between *c.*1710 and 1729, with the exception of the F major concerto by Sammartini, which probably dates from the 1730s.

The concerti were written both for concert use and to provide interval music in the theatres and were popular in the second and third decades of eighteenth-century London: in general they are short exuberant works but of superficial musical content.[60] Fifteen of the concerti were published by Walsh and Hare between *c.*1726 and 1729 (they remained in the catalogue of William Randall, Walsh's successor, and Randall's widow Elizabeth until the late 1770s) and these pieces represent the typical English small flute concerto.[61] Of the three composers whose work was published by Walsh, two had died by 1729 (William Babell in 1723 and Robert Woodcock in 1728) and John Baston appears to have given his final performance in 1733: examination of newspaper announcements and playbills suggests a lessening of interest in the small flute concerti after the middle of the 1720s. In addition to the seventeen concerti, I will also include an untitled anonymous manuscript of a 'suite' preserved in the British Library in A major for sixth flute, two violins, viola and *basso continuo*: the piece is in three movements, two of which are dances and, as such, the piece may be considered more as a suite than a concerto. The concerti of the English composers Babell, Baston, and Woodcock which were published by Walsh share many features in common, whereas the works by the émigré musicians Charles Dieupart and Giuseppe Sammartini and the anonymous suite differ in their orchestration and harmonic development.

Several articles provide information on authorship, orchestration and structure of the concerti, but,

---

59   The term 'flute' implied the recorder, whereas the transverse flute was known as the 'German flute'.

60   Performances of the concerti in theatres and concert rooms are discussed in Chapter 4.

61   John Walsh the elder published between *c.*1692 and 1736, when he was succeeded by his son John Walsh the younger. Most of his music was published in conjunction with John Hare (*fl*1692–1725) and his successor, Joseph. Walsh and Hare were the most prolific publishers of recorder music in early eighteenth-century London. See Charles Humphries and William C. Smith, *Music Publishing in the British Isles*, London: Cassell, 1954), pp.171, 521; *Country Journal or The Craftsman*, 24 February 1731; *London Daily Post and General Advertiser*, 9 August 1739; *A Catalogue of the Vocal and Instrumental Music Printed for, and sold by, William Randall, Successor to the late Mr. John Walsh, in Catherine-Street in the Strand for the year 1776.*

surprisingly, Meierott's *Die kleinen Flötentypen* (1974) makes no significant mention of these pieces.[62] The controversial authorship of Robert Woodcock's concerti is discussed extensively in David Lasocki and Helen Neate's 1988 article and previous speculations made by Brian Priestman in 1954 are rejected.[63] My article in The Consort of 2006, 'The Small Flute Concerto in 18th-Century England', gives a brief outline of the seventeen concerti and the anonymous suite published of the 1720s.[64] Zöe Franklin discusses the harmonic pattern of Babell's concerti in a paper in the Consort of 2007.[65] The orchestration of the small flute concerti and their derivation from Italian-style works is examined in Peter Holman and Richard Maunder's 2000 article in *Early Music*, this discussion being amplified in Maunder's subsequent book.[66] There is no comparative study of the harmonic pattern of the small flute concerti (Franklin's article refers only to Babell), although the orchestration — and the related controversies — of Babell, Baston and Woodcock's concerti is discussed by Maunder: he does not, however, discuss the Sammartini concerto.

3.3. Structure, orchestration, and harmony

The recorder is a relatively soft instrument (consider its French name *flûte douce*) and, whereas sonatas with harpsichord and string bass do not pose problems of audibility, concerti (with their string accompaniment) have to be handled with care to prevent the sound of the recorder being lost in the accompanying ensemble. This problem is particularly acute with alto recorders, which play in the same pitch range as violins, but the use of small recorders, however, overcomes this difficulty and the more penetrating sound of a fifth or sixth flute (or, indeed, a sopranino) is clearly audible above an accompanying string ensemble.

Fifteen of the pieces require a sixth flute, and three require a fifth flute As I have noted, both fifth and sixth flutes are more suited to playing in sharp keys, and only the Sammartini concerto is in a flat key: the major keys employed are D (9), A (4), E (1), F (1), and the minor keys of E minor (1), A minor (1), and B minor (1).[67] Parts for the sixth flute (in D) are written a third higher, and those for the fifth flute (in C) a fourth higher: the fifth and sixth flutes sound an octave higher than written, so a player on a sixth flute reading the note f' (the lowest note on the alto recorder) will be sounding the note d". In addition, transposition of the parts so that the player read alto fingering on a sixth flute had the desirable effect (from the player's perspective) of removing three sharps from the key signature, thus simplifying the fingering and reducing the number of fork-fingerings required. It is curious, however, that Baston chose to use a fifth flute for his sixth concerto in D, but the choice of this instrument for the Dieupart (in A minor) and the Sammartini (in F major) is unremarkable.[68] The use of two sixth flutes in three of the concerti by Woodcock exhibits a parallel with Albinoni's concerti for two oboes and Babell's double concerto has similarities to Pepusch's Opus 8. Two of the concerti have an ambitus of an octave and a fifth, five of an octave and a sixth, and four an octave and a seventh. Two concerti require a two-octave compass, but only one requires the full range of the Baroque recorder, namely an octave and a second: this concerto (Woodcock 1) also requires the difficult note of d-sharp'".[69]

---

62   Lenz Meierott, *Die kleinen Flötentypen*.

63   David Lasocki, and Helen Neate, 'The Life and Works of Robert Woodcock, 1690–1728', *American Recorder*, 24/3 (1988), 92–104; Brian Priestman, 'An Introduction to the Loeillets', *The Consort*, 11 (1954), 18–26; see section 3.4. below.

64   MacMillan, 'The Small Flute Concerto in 18th-Century England', 91–106.

65   Franklin, 'William Babel's [sic] Concertos in Seven Parts', 62–73.

66   Holman and Maunder, 'The Accompaniment of Concertos in 18th-Century England'; Maunder, *The Scoring of Baroque Concertos*.

67   See comments in Chapter 2 regarding the most favourable keys for fifth and sixth flutes.

68   Baston's second and fifth concerti are also in D: Concerto 4 is in A.

69   See below, Chapter 3.4; Woodcock.

All the concerti require an accompaniment of two violins and continuo: ripieno violin parts may be added (three violin parts and/or two viola parts may be encountered in Italian works of the period) but only seven of the small flute concerti require a viola. The soloist(s) may be accompanied by the full ensemble, violin(s) alone or continuo alone — providing textural and dynamic contrast — and there are frequent passages for a solo violin in Babell, Baston and Woodcock's concerti.[70] The instrumental parts may contain the directions 'solo' or 'tutti' but these directions are most probably present to indicate to the players that the subsequent bars are exposed and also that, at that point, any ripienists should drop out. If the ripieno parts did not arise from the composer's hand and were added by Walsh — as suggested by Maunder — the 'solo' and 'tutti' marks were also likely to have been added by Walsh, as Maunder argues that the concerti were likely to have been performed one-to-a-part rather than with a large ensemble. With a large ensemble, only the section leader would play in passages marked 'solo' (as in modern practice), and most publications contained only one copy of each part.[71] However, the question remains open as to how the concerti were accompanied when performed in the theatres which had orchestras often numbering fifteen to twenty players.

The ripieno first violin parts in the small flute concerti are only necessary to provide the harmony in four bars of Woodcock's second concerto, but otherwise serve only to double the principal first violin, either throughout the movement or to reinforce the tutti passages. Rarely, the instrument doubles the second violin (see Table 2). Ripieno second violins are only required in three of Babell's concerti, and again serve to double the second violin throughout the movement or in the tutti passages. The viola is specified in five of the concerti by Babell, Baston and Woodcock, having a part independent of the bass in two (Baston 5 and Woodcock 5). Overall, the ripieno parts may be considered superfluous, and the vast majority of the concerti may be performed with only two violins and bass; a similar situation pertains to the viola, except in two concerti where the instrument does not simply double the bass line. It would seem likely that the extra string parts (which are less demanding than the principal violin parts) were added by Walsh to suit the growing amateur market. Table 2 summarises the parts played by the ripieno violins and viola in the concerti by Babell, Baston, and Woodcock: the concerti by Dieupart and Sammartini have parts only for two violins, viola, and bass, as does the A major suite.[72]

concerto		violino primo ripieno	violino secundo ripieno / viola
Babell 1	i	doubles VP in tuttis	doubles VS in tuttis
	ii	doubles VP throughout	doubles VS throughout
	iii	doubles VP throughout	doubles VS in tuttis
Babell 2	i	tacet	tacet
	ii	25-28 doubles VS· VP in tuttis	doubles VS in tuttis
	iii	doubles VP throughout	doubles VS throughout
	iv	doubles VP throughout	doubles VS throughout
Babell 3	i	tacet	tacet

---

70   Babell 1/i, 4/i, 4/iii; Baston 2/i, 6/i; Woodcock 2/i, 4/i. Baston's first concerto (for alto recorder) has solo violin sections in all three movements, and this concerto also requires a ripieno first violin.

71   Richard Maunder, *The Scoring of Baroque Concertos*, p.131.

72   See section 3.5. for further discussion of the orchestration of Dieupart's concerto.

	ii	doubles VP in tuttis	doubles VS in tuttis
	iii	all four violins in unison: no BC	all four violins in unison
	iv	doubles VP in tuttis	doubles VS in tuttis
Babell 4	i	doubles VP in tuttis	no part in this concerto
	ii	doubles VP throughout (unison)	VS tacet
	iii	doubles VP in tuttis	no part
Baston 2	i	doubles VP in tuttis	viola: doubles bass
	ii	doubles VP throughout	doubles bass
	iii	doubles VP in tuttis	doubles bass
Baston 4	i	all strings in unison with BC[73]	viola: all strings in unison
	ii	doubles VP in tuttis	doubles bass
Baston 5	i	doubles VP in tuttis	viola: independent part
	ii	doubles VP in tuttis	independent part
	iii	doubles VP throughout	independent part
Baston 6	i	doubles VP in tuttis & VS 29-33	viola: doubles bass
	ii	all strings in unison with BC[74]	doubles bass
Woodcock 1	i	doubles VP throughout	no VSR part in this concerto
	ii	doubles VP and VS	
	iii	doubles VP throughout	
Woodcock 2	i	doubles VP in tuttis: needed 19-22	no VSR part in this concerto
	ii	doubles VP and VS (unison)	
	iii	doubles VP and VS	
Woodcock 3	i	doubles VP in tuttis	no VSR part in this concerto
	ii	tacet	
	iii	doubles VPR in tuttis	
Woodcock 4	i	doubles VP in tuttis	no VSR part in this concerto
	ii	doubles VP in tuttis	
	iii	doubles VP in tuttis	

---

73   The bass sounding an octave below the violins.

74   The bass sounding an octave below the violins and viola.

Woodcock 5 i	doubles VP throughout	viola: independent of bass
ii	doubles VP throughout	viola: independent of bass
iii	doubles VP throughout	viola: independent of bass
Woodcock 6 i	doubles VP throughout	no VSR part in this concerto
ii	doubles VP throughout	
iii	doubles VP throughout	

Table 2. Role of the ripieno string parts in the concerti by Babell, Baston, and Woodcock.

The parts for Babell, Baston, and Woodcock's pieces were published by Walsh in complete sets, apparently without the option to purchase (say) extra violin parts, the number of parts being indicated in the title-page (for example, William Babell's 'Concertos in Seven Parts'). Richard Maunder has explored the concept of early eighteenth century concerti for any instrument being accompanied by one-to-a-part strings and finds the evidence compelling, further suggesting that the ripieno parts did not originate from the composers' hands, although no autographs exist.[75] The distribution of the string parts in the Dieupart, Sammartini and the anonymous suite is in the conventional later style with two violins, viola and bass. Several of the concerti contain passages for solo violin, and, from the recorder player's perspective, the pieces are more technically demanding than most of the solo sonatas or duets of the period but — with the exception of the Sammartini — they hardly require a virtuoso technique.

In terms of harmony, the composers restrict themselves — in the main — to the keys described by Michael Talbot in his 1971 paper 'The Concerto Allegro in the Early Eighteenth Century', namely the tonic, dominant, mediant and submediant.[76] For first movements, Talbot suggests three likely arrangements of key sequence in the major keys:

> I V vi I
> I V iii I
> I V vi vii I[77]

and in the minor:

> i III V VI i

These patterns are commonplace — if not universal — in the first movements of the small flute concerti, but the slow movements and concluding fast movements do not demonstrate a consistency of form or harmony. Many of these movements are in binary form; only four concluding movements are in the form of dances, and modulation in these movements is confined to closely related keys.

There are melodies in the concerti which are instantly memorable, whereas others are little more than extended scale or arpeggio passages; many of the solo parts of the concerti consist of arpeggiated passage-work with little development of the melody, although the Sammartini concerto proves an exception. Similar comments may be applied to the frequent violin solos, which are confined to

---

75 Maunder, *The Scoring of Baroque Concertos*, p.131.

76 Michael Talbot, 'The Concerto Allegro in the Early Eighteenth Century', *Music and Letters*, 52/1 (1971), 8–18.

77 Major keys are denoted by upper case figures, minor keys by lower case.

the first violin parts. Opening ritornelli may be repeated in different keys during the course of a movement and often signify a return to the tonic as the movement draws to its conclusion.

The descriptive comments on eighteen works for small recorder(s) and strings require an overall analysis of the features which they exhibit in common and of the features in which they differ. The concerti by Babell, Baston and Woodcock are substantially similar in style and may be considered as one group: the Dieupart, Sammartini and the anonymous suite do not fall easily into this pattern and require an individual discussion. Preceding these discussions, however, salient features regarding choice of recorder, orchestration and harmony are common to most of the works and these are summarised below.

Of the seventeen concerti, twelve are in Vivaldian (fast–slow–fast) three-movement form, whereas three (all by Babell) are in *da chiesa* (slow–fast–slow–fast) form, and two of Baston's concerti have but two movements, although the first movement of Concerto 6 is repeated after the siciliana. Harmonically, Babell's, Baston's and Woodcock's concerti conform broadly to the conventions described by Michael Talbot, modulation being substantially confined to the closely-related keys of the dominant, relative minor and mediant minor (in the major) and to the dominant and relative major in the minor mode.[78]

Of the seventeen, concerti, nine are in D, three in A, and one in E: the keys of E minor, A minor, and B minor are represented by one concerto each, and only the Sammartini lies in the flat key of F. The following table summarises the keys encountered in the fifty-five movements of the concerti:

	I	i	ii	III	iii	IV	iv	V	VI	vi	VII
major	37		3		8	2		34		27	
minor		18		9			3	18	2		1

Table 3. The frequency of the use of keys in the fifty-five movements surveyed (fifteen concerti pieces are written in major keys and three in minor keys).

In the major key concerti, the slow movement is in the relative minor and five of these conclude on a chord of the dominant. The final movements do not follow any set pattern, and only three are written in specific dance forms. Whereas the concerti published by Walsh conform to a conventional — and fairly consistent — pattern, the Dieupart and Sammartini pieces exhibit more extensive modulation: in the case of the Sammartini, this may be explained by its later date of composition, although the Dieupart may date from the 1720s. Both men were accomplished composers, whereas Baston and Woodcock are only known for their handful of concerti. Babell, in this respect, was a more significant composer and also a noted harpsichordist, so it is perhaps surprising that his recorder concerti do not show more extensive harmonic development. The anonymous suite shows similar conventional harmonisation and orchestration to the 'Walsh' concerti, suggesting a similar date of composition.

Babell, Baston and Woodcock's concerti rank amongst the first concerti for solo instrument and strings to be published in England, and evidence from concert notices and playbills suggest that they were composed some years before their publication by Walsh and Hare in the late 1720s. Although tuneful, they are harmonically unadventurous and performance (particularly with one-to-a-part strings) would have posed no problems for the audience to hear the solo small recorder. There are no documented performances of the (later) Sammartini concerto although the Dieupart may have been

---

78   See Tables 2 and 3.

played in London in the 1720s; the A major suite remains in manuscript score. Despite their slight musical content, played as 'interval music' in the theatres as well as in concert rooms, the small flute concerti appear to have been popular with audiences.

Features regarding choice of recorder, orchestration and harmony are common to most of the works and the table below summarises the salient features of the compositions surveyed:

Composer	Flute	Movement	Key	Keys visited	Comments
Babell 1	6	Allegro	D	I V vi I	
		Adagio	b	i III V	
		Allegro	D	I V vi iii I	binary
Babell 2	6	Adagio	D	I V	VP & VS only
		Allegro	D	I V vi iii I V	strings & BC only
		Adagio	D	I V I	
		Allegro	D	I V iii I	binary
Babell 3	6	Adagio	e	i V	ripieno tacet
		Allegro	e	i III V iv I	binary
		Adagio	G	I V IV I	binary; BC tacet
		Allegro	e	i III V i	binary
Babell 4	6	Allegro	A	I V ii vi V I	no VSR in this piece
		Adagio	A	I V IV vi I	rec, VP, VPR only
		Allegro	A	I V vi I	
Babell 5	6 x 2	Adagio	D	I V vi V	
		Allegro	D	I V vi iii I	
		Adagio	b	i V	
		Allegro	D	I V vi I	
Baston 2	6	Allegro	D	I V vi I	
		Adagio	D	I V	
		Presto	D	I vi I	
Baston 4	6	Siciliana	A	I ii vi I	
		Allegro	A	I V vi I	binary
Baston 5	6	Allegro	D	I vi iii V I	
		Andante	b	i III i V	
		Presto	D	I V I	

Baston 6	5	Allegro	D	I vi I	
		Siciliana	D	I V I	da capo
Woodcock 1	6	Presto	E	I V vi I	
		Siciliana	E	I V vi I	binary: BC tacet
		Allegro	E	I V vi iii I	binary
Woodcock 2	6	Allegro	A	I V vi I	
		Adagio	f#	i V	BC tacet
		Minuets	A	I V I	da capo
Woodcock 3	6	Allegro	D	I V vi I	
		Siciliana	b	i V i	binary: BC tacet
		Vivace	D	I V vi iii I	binary
Woodcock 4	6 x 2	Presto	b	i III V i	*devise*
		Largo	b	i V i	
		Gavotte	b	i V iv III i	gavotte; binary
Woodcock 5	6 x 2	Allegro	D	I V vi I	viola
		Largo	b	i III V i	siciliana; binary
		Presto	D	I V vi I	binary
Woodcock 6	6 x 2	Vivace	D	I V vi I	
		Largo	b	i V iv III i	siciliana; binary
		Gavotte	D	I V vi V I	3 gavottes
Dieupart	5	Vivace	a	i VI iv VII V i	
		Grave	a	VI i V	
		Allegro	a	i V i	
Sammartini	5	Allegro	F	I V I / I V iii V	ternary; AA/BB/A
		Siciliana	a	i V III i	
		Allegro	F	I V ii vi iii I	ritornello form; allegro
Anon. suite	6	Allegro	A	I V vi I	allemande; binary
		Andante	f#	i III V	recorder tacet
		Minuet	A	I V I	binary

Table 4. Synopsis of the small flute concerti

3.4. The concerti by Babell, Baston, and Woodcock

William Babell

William Babell was born in London *c*.1690 and died on 23 September 1723.[79] He was the son of a bassoonist and studied with Johann Christoph Pepusch: it is possible that he may also have studied with Handel. Babell's principal claim to fame lies in his ability as a keyboard player, being a noted harpsichordist but he played the violin in the band of King George I: he played the harpsichord in various theatre orchestras and published virtuosic arrangements of operatic arias and overtures, demonstrating his skill in ornamentation.[80] For the last five years of his life, he was organist of All Hallows, Bread Street, where he was succeeded by the blind John Stanley. Hawkins linked Babell with Robert Woodcock as a composer of recorder concerti and Johann Gottfried Walther's *Musicalisches Lexicon* of 1732 described the (by then) late Babell as a famous keyboard player and composer.[81] His sole surviving contribution to the recorder repertoire is a set of six concerti, which were published posthumously by Walsh and Hare as the composer's Opus 3 in 1726:

> Babell's/CONCERTOS/ in 7 Parts:/The first four for VIOLINS and one small Flute/ and the two last for VIOLINS and two FLUTES./The proper Flute being nam'd to each CONCERTO. Compos'd by the Late/Mr. WILLm. BABELL./Performed at the Theatre with great applause./Opera Terza./

Walsh wrote an elaborate tribute to the composer in the first recorder part:

> 'The Occasion of this Preface, was to congratulate the Harmonious on the Publication of this work, Compos'd by my late lov'd Friend, Mr. WILLIAM BABELL.
> 'The following Pieces being obtain'd from the Executors of a particular friend of the Author's, I hope will prove an Example to induce all Persons, who have any other of his compositions, to oblidge [*sic*] the Public with them.
> 'When the world is so unfortunate as to lose an esteemed Author, the only consolation we have, is the enjoyment of his Works: therefore 'tis to be hoped that notwithstanding, the too common Vanity of making manuscripts scarce, by confineing [*sic*] to the Closets of Particulars; it will in this case be avoided.
> 'HARMONY is so Universally esteem'd, that to conceal any of his Performances, would be in some measure doing an Injustice to the Public: Burying a Treasure that might be enjoy'd by others without loss to the Donor: and denying him that Beautifull and lasting Monument which his Genius has rais'd him to in his works,
> In fine, our Author may justly be Recorded, an Inexhaustible Treasure of Harmony, and, had he lived in SHAKESPEARE'S time;
> We might justly have concluded him the Occasion of the following lines.
> > If music be the Food of Love, play on;
> > That strain again; it had a dying Fall;
> > Oh! It came o're my ear like a sweet Sound
> > That breathes upon a Bank of Violets
> > Stealing and giving Odours
> > > > SHAK.

---

79   His name is sometimes spelt 'Babel'.

80   Gerald Gifford and Terence Best, 'Babell, William' *Grove Music Online, Oxford Music Online*, http://www.oxfordmusiconline.com, (Oxford: Oxford University Press, 2007–2016, accessed 19 August 2015).

81   John Hawkins, *A General History of the Science and Practice of Music*, vol.5, note, p.180.

Whilst this may be a heartfelt testimony to one who died young, it rather suggests that Walsh was touting for business, and makes its own comment upon the publisher's English; Hawkins, for one, considered Walsh to be illiterate.

The first four concerti require one sixth flute, the fifth requires two sixth flutes and the sixth is written for two alto recorders and is therefore excluded from discussion here. No autograph survives, leading to a degree of speculation regarding the date of composition of the music. In the lists of the effects of the 'musical small coals man', Thomas Britton (who died in 1714), there is mention of '12 Concertos by Dr. Pepusch, young Mr. Babel and Vivaldi', and Richard Maunder suggests that it is possible that one or more of the concerti mentioned could be the recorder concerti.[82] As far as is known Babell did not publish any other concerti, lending a degree of credibility to this statement. Maunder suggests that Concerti 5 and 6 (for two recorders) could date from as early as c.1710 in view of their similarity to Pepusch's Opus 8 concerti but considers that the remaining four possibly date from c.1715.[83] Holman and Maunder consider that the recorder concerti (including Babell's works) are amongst the first English compositions in the genre. The earliest documented performance of a Babell concerto took place on 12 March 1718, as announced in the *Daily Courant* of 10 March 1718.[84] The notice, however, does not specify which of Babell's concerti were performed, or even confirm that it was for the recorder. Zöe Franklin discusses the hypothesis that the concerti may have been developed by Walsh from trio sonatas, but she 'does not find the evidence convincing'.[85] I would concur with Franklin, in that, if the ripieno string parts are excluded, Babell, Baston and Woodcock's concerti all belong to the same genre of concerto for recorder, two violins, and basso continuo. The peculiarities of the ripieno string parts (see Table 1) suggest that they are not of the composer's making, but, as I have noted, no autograph is extant. In comparison with Baston's concerti there are relatively few documented performances of the Babell works, although the title-page notes that they were 'Perform'd at the theatre with great applause': however, evidence to confirm Walsh's assertion is lacking. At Hickford's Rooms on 16 April 1729 a benefit concert for the celebrated oboist Jack Kytch included a 'Concerto for the little flute composed by Babell'. Kytch would have been the soloist.[86]

Concerti 1 and 4 are written in Vivaldian three-movement style (fast–slow–fast), whereas the remainder conform to a slow–fast–slow–fast pattern. The movements are all assigned the tempo marks of either adagio or allegro. Some of the movements are designated ₵, suggesting duple time (2/2) rather than the common time signature of C (4/4) which the pulse of the music suggests; citing *The Compleat Flute*-Master, Robert Donington points out, however, that C implies a slower motion than ₵, which would explain the apparent anomaly in the time-signature.[87] The lawyer, amateur musician and commentator on music Roger North (1651–1734) concurs; 'The old mark of Comon

---

82   Maunder, *The Scoring of Baroque Concertos*, p.113; Britton's effects were listed by Hawkins in his *A General History*, vol.5, pp.79–88: Babell's concerti are listed in item 102; no other concerti by Babell are listed in *New Grove II*.

83   *VI Concerts à 2 Flûtes à Bec, 2 Flûtes Traversieres haubois ou Violons & Basse Continue*, Op.8 (Roger, Amsterdam,1717): although published by Roger in 1717, the pieces are probably of an earlier date (Maunder, *The Scoring of Baroque Concertos*, p.117); Maunder, *ibid.*, p.119.

84   Holman and Maunder, 'The Accompaniment of Concertos in 18th-Century England'; 'At the Tennis Court in the Haymarket was performed 'A new Overture, compos'd by Mr Babel [*sic*], with a Solo on the Harpsichord, to be perform'd by him. A new Cantata, and other Concerto's [*sic*] by the same Master...' *The Daily Courant*, 10 March 1718, cited in Maunder *The Scoring of Baroque Concertos*, p.120.

85   Franklin, 'Babel's *Concertos in 7 Parts*'.

86   Michael Tilmouth, 'A Calendar of References to Music in Newspapers published in London and the Provinces (1660–1719)', *Royal Musical Association Research Chronicle*, 1 (1961), 1–107.

87   Robert Donington, *The Interpretation of Early Music* (London: Faber and Faber, 1975), p.410; concerto 1/i, iii, concerto 2/ii, concerto 3/ii, concerto 5/ii.

[*sic*] Time, quickening, C, ₵, (etc.).'[88]

The 'seven parts' comprise the solo flute (recorder), 'violino primo', 'violino primo ripieno', 'violino secundo', 'violino secundo ripieno' and two copies of the basso continuo.[89] The disposition of the violin parts — with ripieno instruments — is unusual, and Maunder suggests that the ripieno violin parts may originate from Walsh's 1726 publication rather than from Babell's hand:

> Probably the ripieno violins were added by Walsh to suit a later taste, for they never have independent parts but just double the first and second versions in a rather random fashion. The parts cannot be right as they stand: in No.1, for example, most solos are accompanied by a bassetto assigned to violins 1, 2 and ripieno violin 1, while ripieno violin 2 absurdly has rests; and in the finale of No.2 a passage for violin 1 in imitation with the soloist is duly marked *solo* but is nevertheless doubled by the ripieno part.[90]

Maunder further comments that it is surprising that Concerto 4 has only one ripieno violin part and adds that 'it is doubtful whether violins were meant to be doubled in works without viola'.[91] Arthur Hutchings noted that there was a shortage of viola players in eighteenth-century England, although this may or may not be relevant to Babell's work.[92] In practice, there is little to be gained by adding ripieno violins as they do not have significant independent parts and do not add to the harmony.

In terms of harmony, Babell restricts himself — in the main — to the keys described by Talbot in his 1971 paper on 'The Concerto Allegro in the Early Eighteenth Century'. Whereas Babell does not entirely follow the sequences described retrospectively in Talbot's twentieth-century commentary, he does adhere to the keys, with only rare excursions to the subdominant. Franklin observes that Babell's compositions tend to be less symmetrical in form than those of the Italian master, Corelli.[93] She further comments on Babell's repeated use of his opening ritornello passages to confirm the tonal centre. Many of his melodies, however, amount to little more than extended passage-work with frequent imitative scale and arpeggio passages: in this respect his concerti are perhaps less interesting than those of his contemporaries, Baston and Woodcock.

The four solo small flute concerti by William Babell are early examples of the English solo concerto form, and were not published (as far as is known) until three years after the composer's death. Like the concerti by Baston and Woodcock (discussed below) they were possibly played as interval music in the theatre as well as in concert rooms; unlike Baston and Woodcock, however, there is no evidence that Babell was a recorder player. The orchestration of the concerti (as published by Walsh) is questionable, and all the pieces can be satisfactorily performed with recorder(s), two violins and continuo.

The first concerto (in D) is an unremarkable three-movement work, whereas the second concerto (also in D) is in four-movement form, the opening eight-bar adagio being scored for two violins alone. The recorder is similarly excluded from the following allegro for violins and continuo, but the final two movements are unremarkable. David Lasocki and Anthony Rowland-Jones consider this work to be a hybrid: 'a curious combination of concerto grosso and solo concerto'. They comment that only the finale is conventional in its treatment of recorder and orchestra, although I find little that is unconventional — structurally, melodically, or harmonically — in the third movement (adagio).[94]

---

88   John Wilson (ed.), *Roger North on Music* (London: Novello, 1959), p.99.

89   In the following discussion, I shall abbreviate these terms to 'VP', 'VPR', 'VS', 'VSR' and 'BC'.

90   Maunder, *The Scoring of Baroque Concertos*, p.124.

91   Maunder, *The Scoring of Baroque Concertos*, p.124.

92   Arthur Hutchings, *The Baroque Concerto* (London: 2nd edn., Faber and Faber, 1972), p.330.

93   Franklin, 'Babel's *Concertos in 7 Parts*'.

94   David Lasocki and Anthony Rowland-Jones, 'The Eighteenth-Century Recorder Concerto' in *The Cambridge Companion to the Recorder*, ed. by John Mansfield Thomson (Cambridge: Cambridge University Press, 1995), p.115.

The third and fourth concerti (in E minor and A respectively) conform to a conventional pattern.

The final concerto of the set for two sixth flutes is worthy of more detailed consideration.
In this four-movement work, oboes may be substituted for violins. This is the only Babell concerto to incorporate oboes, but the second oboe part calls for the notes of c-sharp' eighteen times and b, thrice: these notes are not obtainable on the two- or three-keyed oboe of the early eighteenth century.[95] It seems unlikely that a composer of Babell's stature would not have known the compass of the oboe of his day, and it is certainly possible that the idea of substituting oboes for violins could have derived from Walsh. The oboe parts are alternatives to the violins, rather than playing separate material. Maunder suggests that this concerto may originally have been written for two alto recorders (as is the F major Concerto 6) and transposed down a minor third to be playable an octave higher on sixth flutes.[96] If this is indeed the case, the violin/oboe parts would lie comfortably on an early eighteenth-century oboe. Organologically this makes sense, for there appears to be no other English music assigned to two sixth flutes in the early years of the eighteenth century and it would explain the peculiar disposition of the oboe parts and the appearance of the note AA (a careless copying error) in the bass in the penultimate bar of the final movement. It does, however, pose the questions as to why the concerto was transposed without attention to the compass of the instruments for which it was composed and why the sixth concerto was not similarly transposed. The sixth concerto is written in F and, with downward transposition of a minor third, the parts could be played on sixth flutes sounding an octave higher. There is a marked similarity in the scoring between this piece and some of the allegro movements in Pepusch's Opus 8 concerti, which would tend to suggest that the fifth Babell concerto may have been written earlier than the solo concerti. The Pepusch concerti also present the possibility of using two contrasting pairs of wind instruments, with violins as an alternative.[97] Harmonically, the Pepusch and Babell concerti both exhibit conventional modulatory patterns, and in both pieces the third movement lies in the relative minor key and concludes on a chord of the dominant. The recorder and violin pairs often play in parallel thirds, or with the first players in unison (and similarly the seconds), or as alternating sections with recorders and violins accompanied by the continuo, following the pattern of the Pepusch's opus 8 concerti. There are no ripieno violin parts.

It should be recalled that Babell studied with Pepusch, and this fact may shed some light on the structure of concerti 5 and 6.

John Baston

John Baston came from a musical family; his date of birth is not known, but his name is first encountered in a record of a concert given at Stationers' Hall, London, in 1709 when he performed a concerto grosso with his violinist brother, Thomas (fl1708–27).[98] John was employed at the Lincoln's Inn Fields Theatre as a 'cellist between 1714 and 1722, after which he moved to the Theatre Royal in Drury Lane. Although primarily a 'cellist, he was also an accomplished recorder player and composer and performed his recorder concerti (often in conjunction with his violinist brother) as 'interval music' between plays in the theatres. Baston's name frequently appeared in playbills, and he appears to have been very popular with audiences. Charles Burney described him in the context of 'favourite

95   Anthony Baines, *Woodwind Instruments and Their History* (London: Faber and Faber, corrected 3rd. edn, 1977, repr. New York: Dover, 1991), p.282.

96   Maunder, *The Scoring of Baroque Concertos*, p.120.

97   Pepusch, *VI Concerts à 2 Flûtes à Bec, 2 Flûtes Traversieres Haubois ou Violons & Basse Continue*, Op.8; see note 83 above.

98   *Daily Courant*, 24 August 1709.

musicians of our own country at this time' as 'Baston on the common-flute'.[99] His last documented performance took place in Drury Lane in 1733 and he was one of the founder patrons of the Society of Musicians; he is said to have died in 1739. A Miss Baston was on the staff of the Theatre Royal Covent Garden, as a harpsichordist and a dancer in the 1730s, and it is tempting to think she may have been the daughter of John or Thomas. John Baston's surviving compositions amount to a set of six concerti for the recorder, the second of which was arranged for two flutes and published in *The Delightful Companion* in 1745.[100] This volume also contains a sixteen-bar fragment for two flutes by 'Mr. Baston', which is not found in any of the concerti.

John Baston's

> Six/CONCERTOS/in Six Parts/for VIOLINS and FLUTES/viz. a Fifth, Sixth and Consort Flute./The Proper Flute being nam'd to each/CONCERTO

were published by Walsh and Hare in 1729. However, Walsh continued to advertise Baston's concerti at least until 1731, when an advertisement in the *Country Journal and General Advertiser* proclaimed the concerti of Babell, Baston and Woodcock.[101]

> Like Babell's concerti, they continued to appear publishers' catalogues until the 1770s.[102]

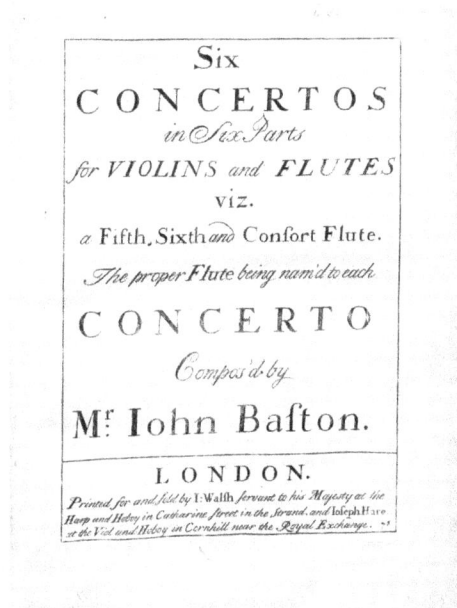

Figure 3. Title-page of Walsh's edition of Baston's concerti[103]

The first, second, and fifth concerti are in Vivaldian three-movement form, whereas the third, fourth

---

99   For example: 7 May 1716 'The Confederacy' A concerto for the violin and flute, to be performed by Mr Baston and his brother; Charles Burney, *A General History of Music*, vol.2, ed. Frank Mercer (New York: Dover, 1957), p.1001.

100   John Simpson (publisher), *THE DELIGHTFUL/Pocket Companion/for the/GERMAN FLUTE… PRINTED for/& sold by John Simpson* (London: John Simpson, 1745), 8, 30: The volume contains solos and duets for the transverse flute.

101   *Daily Post*, 2 April 1729; *Country Journal or The Craftsman*, 24 February 1731.

102   See note 61, above.

103   ©The British Library Board, shelfmark i.53. Title-page

and fifth have only two movements. The third (for alto recorder) and sixth concerti, however, require the first movement to be repeated after the slow movement, effectively making them three-movement works. The instruction 'Da Capo' is written after the Adagio (second movement) of Concerto 3 for alto recorder and 'end with the Allegro' after the Siciliana of Concerto 6. In the absence of an autograph score, it is not possible to determine whether the instruction to repeat the first movements emanated from the composer or the publisher. The first violin parts of Concerti 1, 2 and 6 (which may have been written for the composer's brother) contain solo passages for the instrument.

The first and third concerti are scored for the consort flute (alto recorder), the second, fourth and fifth for the sixth flute, and sixth concerto for the fifth flute. Baston stipulates three violin parts, VP, VPR (here spelt 'repiano'), VS, 'tenore', and bass.[104] It is only in the first concerto that VPR has a significant part; elsewhere it doubles VP (and, very occasionally, VS) in the tutti passages. As Baston's concerti were most commonly performed in the theatres which employed orchestras, it is possible that the ripieno parts were intended for ripienists in the orchestra, but, equally, they could have been added by Walsh, possibly for amateur domestic use. There are several apparent errors in the parts. The 'tenore' (viola) part doubles the bass at the octave, or occasionally plays in unison with it, except in Concerto 5: the part is notated in the alto clef in Concerti 1, 3, and 5 but in the mezzo-soprano clef in Nos. 2, 4, and 6. In Concerti 1, 3, and 5, however, the part occasionally lies below the lowest note of the viola, namely c.[105] Susi Möhlmeier and Frédéric Thouvenot, commenting on the string parts, write about '[the] tenore [part] corresponding to the alto [viola] part but with a string going down to G, a fourth lower' suggesting an unconventional tuning.[106] I would speculate that Baston *may* have been writing for the rare tenor violin (tuning G, d, a, e') but concur with Maunder's opinion that it is more likely that the copyist was lacking in care when he prepared the parts.[107] Baston tends to adhere to the tonal patterns described by Talbot: his concerti are unpretentious, tuneful works. Apart from Concerto 5, the viola is supplementary, and a ripieno violin is only necessary in Concerto 1 for alto recorder; the prominent first violin parts may have been intended for Baston's brother Thomas. As Concerti 1 and 3 are written for the alto recorder, they are not further discussed here.

Baston's second concerto is unremarkable, but the fourth (in A) is a curious two-movement work but, unlike concertos 3 and 6, there is no indication that the allegro should be repeated to form a three-movement piece. Maunder suggests that this concerto 'appears to have been cobbled together from a Siciliana for recorder and continuo (…) and a short trio sonata movement for "sixth flute", violin and continuo'.[108] Certainly the fourth concerto does not bear the marks of a thoroughly-composed concerto (unlike the remainder of Baston's output, copyist's errors excluded) and I would concur with Maunder that the work has been 'cobbled together' although the previous sources of the piece are not known. The orchestration of the Siciliana is unorthodox in that the violins play in unison throughout and double the bass at the octave. The presence of the note BB in the bass (bars 8 and 16 of the Siciliana) suggest either transposition of a previous work or copyist's error, and the absence of repeat signs in the allegro (which appears to be in binary form) is also likely to be an error.

In the fifth concerto in D, the 'tenore' (viola) part is (unusually) largely independent of the bass: in the final chord of the andante, the part requires the note A which lies a third below the range of the viola when using conventional tuning. The final concerto of the set is scored for the fifth flute, despite being in the home key of the sixth flute (Concerti 2 and 5 are in D, and require the sixth flute). The reason for this is not apparent, for the work presents no particular technical difficulty in

---

104   Compare with the orchestration of Babell's concerti as outlined above.

105   In Concerti 1 and 3 to G, in Concerto 5 to A.

106   Susi Möhlmeier and Frédéric Thouvenot, 'Introduction to Jean Marc Fuzeau's facsimile edition of John Baston's *Six Concertos (1729*, ed. Jean Marc Fuzeau (Courlay; Fouzeau, 1997), p.IX.

107   Sybil Marcuse, *A Survey of Musical Instruments* (New York: Harper & Row, 1975), p.532; Maunder, *The Scoring of Baroque Concertos*, pp.122–3.

108   Maunder, *The Scoring of Baroque Concertos*, p.123.

the transposed key of G, rather than the transposed key of F in Concerti 2 and 5, and the part lies within the compass of either the fifth or sixth flute. Examination of the score reveals that VPR is unnecessary — as is the viola, which in this case doubles the bass. The modulation is confined to very closely-related keys.

Robert Woodcock

Robert Woodcock was born in London in 1690 (he was baptised on 9 October of that year) and died in London on 28 April 1628, supposedly of gout. The engraver George Vertue (1684–1756) commented that 'besides this his great genius to musick which studyd [sic] at times, so as to compose pieces of musick of many parts, for several instruments that are well approved off [sic] by Masters of Musick, playing a part himself'.[109] Although a fine marine painter and amateur musician (playing the recorder and oboe as well as composing), Woodcock worked in government service for most of his life before abandoning his clerk's desk for the painter's easel in 1723. Sadly, he died in poverty. Woodcock was an admirer of the celebrated Dutch marine painter Willem van de Velde II (1633–1707), who lived in London from 1673 until his death and Woodcock imitated the Dutchman's style; three of his paintings (of high quality) are conserved at the National Maritime Museum, Greenwich, London.[110] Hawkins, writing in 1776, described Woodcock as 'a celebrated performer' on the flute and also discussed the transposition of the recorder parts in the concerti although there is no surviving contemporary record of Woodcock himself performing in public.[111]

Woodcock's sole surviving compositions form a set of twelve concerti published by Walsh and Hare in 1727, although they may have been written as early as 1722.[112] Of these, the first six are relevant to the present study, those for oboe and German flute being excluded.

> XII CONCERTOS/in Eight Parts/The first three for/VIOLINS and one Small FLUTE/The Second three for/VIOLINS and two Small FLUTES/The third three for/VIOLINS & One GERMAN FLUTE/and the three last for/VIOLINS/& one HOBOY/The proper Flute Being nam'd to each Concerto/Compos'd by ROBERT WOODCOCK.

In 1954, Brian Priestman published an article in *The Consort* suggesting that Woodcock was not the composer of the concerti published by Walsh and Hare, but that he was a painter who, while travelling in the Low Countries, had appropriated works by Jacques Loeillet (1685–1748) and had these published in London under his own name.[113] Carl Dolmetsch concurred with this theory and suggested that Woodcock was not the composer and recorder player described by Hawkins, but was

---

109   *The Twenty-Second Volume of the Walpole Society. Vertue Note Books*, Volume III (Oxford: Oxford University Press, 1934), p.23.

110   Accession numbers BHC0982, BHC0983, BHC0984.

111   Hawkins, *A General History of the Science and Practice of Music*, vol.4, note, p.131: '...the method was to write the flute part in a key corresponding to its pitch; this practice was introduced by one Woodcock, a celebrated performer on this instrument, and by an ingenious young man, William Babell, organist of the church of Allhallows Bread-street, London, about the year 1710, both of whom published concertos for this instrument, in which the principal part was for a sixth flute, in which case the lowest note, though nominally F, was in the power D, and consequently required a transposition of the flute-part a sixth higher, viz., into the key of D'. It should be noted that such transposition had been practised in the late seventeenth century.

112   *London Journal*, 18 February 1727; the *Daily Courant* of 13 March 1722 gave notice of a concert at Drury Lane the following day which would include 'A New Concerto on the little Flute, compos'd by Mr. Woodcocke [sic] and perform'd by Mr John Baston'. If this were one of the twelve concerti it would indicate a date of composition some five years before Walsh published the music.

113   Brian Priestman, 'An Introduction to the Loeillets', *The Consort*, 11 (1954), 18–26.

a celebrated marine painter who copied the works of van de Velde and who happened also to be an amateur musician.[114] Priestman based his assertion on the similarity of Woodcock's third concerto to a manuscript copy of a flute concerto by Loeillet in Brussels (itself a copy of a manuscript in the University of Rostock). I examined the Rostock manuscript some years ago, and observed that, although the outer movements of the Rostock piece were virtually identical to the Walsh edition of 1727, the central movement was different (see music example below). In the Rostock copy, the slow movement is a *grave* in common time, the recorder being accompanied by unison violins and continuo, whereas the Walsh edition has a siciliana with accompaniment by unison violins alone, a feature of all Woodcock's concerti for solo recorder.[115] In addition, the solo part in the Rostock manuscript is written in the tonic key and not transposed to suit the player of a sixth flute using alto fingering.

Ex.6. Woodcock, 3ʳᵈ concerto for sixth flute, 2ⁿᵈ movement, siciliana, bars 1–4.
Pub. John Walsh, 1720s. Dolmetsch Library of Early Music, Haslemere.

Ex.6. Flute concerto ascr. Loeillet, 2ⁿᵈ movement, grave, bars 1-3.
Brussels/University of Rostock.

Music example. Woodcock, 3/ii, contrasting the Haslemere/Walsh version (above) and the Brussels/Rostock version (below).[116]

I concluded that Priestman's ascription to Loeillet was improbable, and more recent work by David Lasocki and Helen Neate, in a more extensive study of Woodcock's life and works, confirmed my hypothesis.[117] The last documented performance of a Woodcock concerto took place in 1734 but Walsh was still advertising Woodcock's concerti (together with those of Babell) in 1739, and the concerti (together with those of Babell and Baston) remained in the catalogue of Walsh's successor William Randall, as late as 1776.[118] A set of parts for the concerti were purchased from Walsh in 1754 for use in the Dublin charity concerts.[119]

Concerti 1, 2, 3, 4 and 6 conform basically to a Vivaldian three-movement form, with many solo passages accompanied only by a violin bassetto. David Lasocki considers that Concerto 5 is more Handelian in character (although still in three-movement form), noting that the construction and melodic material are more Handelian than Vivaldian.[120] Woodcock's concerti are scored for VP, VPR, VS, viola (of the recorder concerti, in Concerto 5 only) and BC. The 'eight parts' of the title page

114   Carl Dolmetsch, conversation with MacMillan, 1983.

115   Douglas MacMillan, 'A New Concerto, Compos'd by Mr. Woodcock', *Recorder and Music Magazine*, (1985), 180–181.

116   Reproduced from MacMillan. 'The Small Flute Concerto', *The Consort*, 62 (2006), p.99, by permission of the editor.

117   David Lasocki and Helen Neate, 'The Life and Works of Robert Woodcock, 1690–1728' *American Recorder*, 24/3 (1988), 92–104.

118   See note 62, above.

119   Denis Arnold, 'Charity Music in 18ᵗʰ-Century Dublin, *Galpin Society Journal*, 11 (1968), 162–174.

120   Lasocki and Neate, *op. cit.*

include two bass parts (one figured) and one or two solo recorders: it is only Concerto 5 that contains all eight parts. Woodcock provides dynamic contrast by having four patterns of orchestration: solo recorder(s), recorder(s) with unison violins, recorder with continuo, and the full ensemble. Except in Concerto 2, VPR is not essential, merely doubling VP but having rests in the solo passages; similarly, the viola is only required in the fifth. In the three concerti for solo recorder, the accompaniment in the slow movement is provided by violins alone, a feature found also in Babell's fourth concerto and in works by Vivaldi. Woodcock's concerti were all written for sixth flute(s) and harmonically they follow conventional early eighteenth-century patterns; the solo parts require a fine technique, but, like Babell's and Baston's works, they could hardly be described as demanding great virtuosity.

The three solo concerti are all written in sharp keys (E, A, and D) and the first movement of Concerto 1 requires the note f-sharp''' (notated transposed, in reality d-sharp''') on two occasions in the opening allegro. This note is not easily obtainable on the Baroque recorder (#XIV/♭XV) and it is surprising to find it required an English concerto. The second concerto is notable for the only use in Woodcock's output of VPR being necessary to maintain the harmony:

It is to the third solo concerto that I made reference when discussing the disputed authorship of Woodcock's concerti: see music example 2 above. This concerto is otherwise unremarkable.

In the three concerti for two sixth flutes (numbers 4, 5, and 6) the recorders frequently play in thirds. The fourth concerto is only one of three small flute concerti in a minor key (B minor, but again in a sharp key): in the largo there are blocks of minim chords on beats 1 and 2, followed by a crotchet rest and crotchet pattern throughout the movement, suggesting a lilting sarabande-like rhythm, and the final gavotte seems disproportionally brief. The fifth concerto is the only concerto of the set to require a viola, the part for which is more aligned with the violins than the bass. In the sixth concerto, the final gavotte is presented in three iterations of increasing melodic complexity, although the harmony could best be described as basic.

Summary

The fifteen concerti composed by Babell, Baston, and Woodcock and published by Walsh exhibit many similarities. Their harmonic structure is elementary with the major key movements almost exclusively lying in closely-related keys and the supertonic and subdominant only feature briefly in three out of forty-six movements. Three of the concerti are in four movement form, two in two movements, whilst the remaining nine conform to the fast – slow – fast configuration. The conundrum of the ripieno string parts has been discussed above, and it seems most probably that these were added by the publisher, but the solo violin parts would appear to be original. Accompaniment of the solo recorder in the slow movement of four of the concerti is provided by violins alone, and the one use of oboes (in Babell's double concerto) is problematic. Melodically, the concerti vary from repetitive scale and arpeggio passages with limited development to instantly-memorable tunes, and, on a technical level, these concerti could hardly be described as virtuosic, and could be performed successfully by competent amateurs.

3.5. The concerti by Dieupart, Sammartini, and an anonymous suite

Charles Dieupart

Charles, also known as François, Dieupart (c.1667–c.1740) was a French-born composer and harpsichordist who arrived in England c.1703. He was closely associated with both the Theatre Royal, Drury Lane, and The Queen's Theatre as a harpsichordist and he also published keyboard suites with alternative versions for violin or recorder with continuo. Dieupart left five concerti, including a small flute concerto (which apparently was not published) in A minor. On 11 May 1722, *The Daily Courant* advertised 'a Concerto for the little Flute composed by Monsieur Dieupart, and performed by Mr. Baston and others' at Drury Lane, and (in the absence of other recorder concerti by Dieupart) this could be assumed to be the A minor concerto.[121] Maunder suggests the date of composition as 'the early 1720s', presumably on the evidence provided by this performance but no autograph or English edition is extant, although the concerto exists in manuscript parts in Dresden.[122] Maunder describes the distribution of these parts as being 'in the Dresden manner'.[123] The concerto is in three movements, and appears in two separate manuscript hands, the first written for *Flauto o Hautbois*, two violins, viola, *violone grosso*, harpsichord, two oboes, and bassoon. The woodwind parts essentially double the strings. In the second hand (for *flautino* and four violins) there are no woodwind parts and the solo part notated in the French (G1) violin clef with transposition to D minor, indicating a fifth flute. The large orchestra with woodwind parts doubling the strings is not found in any other English small flute concerto, and Fiona Smith has suggested to me that a copy of the concerto (probably with string accompaniment only) arrived in Dresden, and local musicians added the woodwind parts to suit the Dresden court orchestra.[124] Harmonically, there is more extensive modulation than is to be found in Babell, Baston, and Woodcock's music, perhaps because Dieupart was a notable harpsichordist rather than an amateur composer (Woodcock) or a player-composer (Baston).

Discussing the authorship of the piece in the preface to his edition of the concerto (with keyboard reduction), David Lasocki comments that certain stylistic features of the slow movement bear a similarity to two of Babell's concerti. He writes 'This movement begins with two fast, unmeasured flourishes in the recorder part, continued by a slow-moving melodic line. The accompaniment is basically in quarter notes'.[125] The second movement of Babell's first concerto has a crotchet accompaniment and also ends on the chord of the dominant (as does the third movement of Concerto 2) and Concerto 4 has a lyrical melody over a quaver accompaniment provided by unison violins. The similarities (which are not substantial) are in style rather than harmony, and are not exclusive to Babell and Dieupart.

Despite the atypical harmony of the first movement (at least in comparison with Babell, Baston, and Woodcock) and with due consideration of the orchestration, there appears to be no convincing reason why this piece by a French *emigré* to England and who did not actually work in Dresden should not be ranked with the English small flute concerti of the 1720s.

---

121   *The Daily Courant*, 11 May 1722.

122   D–Dl Mus. 2174–0–1.

123   Maunder, The Scoring of Baroque Concertos, p.129.

124   Fiona Smith, email to MacMillan, 11 June 2019.

125   David Lasocki, 'Preface' in F. Dieupart, *Concerto in A minor for Soprano Recorder with Piano Reduction* (Tokyo: Zen-on Music, R-154, 1979), p.154-4.

Giueseppe Sammartini

The sole surviving manuscript of this concerto is preserved in the Musik och Teaterbiblioteket in Stockholm.[126] The manuscript is headed 'Concerto a piu Istromenti per la Fluta. Di Giusep.° St. Martini'. The composer was a distinguished oboist (born in 1695) who arrived in London around 1728 and died there in 1750. His compositions (described by Burney as 'full of science, originality, and fire') are mainly instrumental and, although he wrote for the flute, the present concerto appears to be his only work for small recorder.[127]

The concerto is scored for recorder (the transposition of the part indicating the fifth flute or soprano recorder), four-part strings and continuo.[128] The recorder may be unaccompanied (for short periods only), accompanied by violins, or continuo; the viola line is independent of the bass and does not join with the violins when they alone accompanying the recorder. 'There are solo and tutti marks in the string parts , and on two instances the bass line is marked Violonc. Solo, indicating accompaniment by the string bass without the harpsichord.

The concerto is in three movements, the first in ternary form (unique in the English small flute concerti), and a siciliana is followed by an allegro assai. Technically, this is the most demanding movement (perhaps the most technically demanding movement in all the small flute concerti) with rapid semiquaver passage-work, chromatic semitones and written-out cross-fingered trills.

The piece is on a larger scale than the concerti of Babell, Baston and Woodcock: it is technically more demanding, and, in the words of Clas Pehrsson, 'falls between the late Baroque and pre-Classical periods'.[129] It is likely to date from a later period than the previously-mentioned works, but there are no records of its being performed in the eighteenth century. Despite postulating a date of composition of 'the late 1720s or 30s', Lasocki and Rowland-Jones note that 'there are many chromatic touches, verging on the *empfindsam*' but, to my mind, this would suggest a date of perhaps later than the 1730s.[130] Sammartini, as an oboist, may well have played the recorder and it is tempting to speculate that he may have performed the concerto himself.

Anonymous suite in A for sixth flute

The British Library Add.MS 31453 contains an untitled 'suite' of three movements (allemanda, andante and minuet) for sixth flute, two violins, viola, and *basso continuo* by an unknown composer.[131] The manuscript is undated, but the presence of an allemande and minuet and both the style of the

---

126 S–Skma FbO-R.

127 By the third decade of the eighteenth century the term 'flute' would probably be applied in England either to the transverse flute or the recorder, although the latter is more likely. Although Sammartini's sonatas and trio sonatas are often adapted for the recorder, they were written for the transverse flute. However, a manuscript in the Sibley Music Library, Eastman School of Music, Rochester, contains twenty-seven sonatas for flute, oboe, recorder and violin, fourteen being assigned to the alto recorder; Burney, *A General History of Music*, p.1001.

128 The parts listed on the wrapper to the score are listed as Flauto concerto, due violini, viola, basso.

129 Clas Pehrsson, liner note in Clas Pehrsson and the Drottingholm Baroque Ensemble '*Recorder Concerti*' (Grammofon AB Bis CD-210, 1982 & 1986).

130 David Lasocki and Anthony Rowland-Jones, 'The Eighteenth-Century Recorder Concerto' in *The Cambridge Companion to the Recorder*, p.110.

131 I am indebted to the late Dr Walter Bergmann for drawing my attention to this music, and for providing me with a score and continuo realisation taken from the original in the British Library. Dr Bergmann has transposed the recorder part into the tonic key so that it may be played on a soprano recorder using standard fingering. The manuscript is notated in C, appropriate for the sixth flute played with alto fingering.

music and its harmonic structure would suggest that it is of early eighteenth-century origin.

It has been suggested that the suite may have been composed by Peter Prelleur (*c*.1705 – 41) on account of its supposed similarity to a trumpet concerto in Dresden.[132] I do not perceive, however, sufficient similarity between the Prelleur concerto and the A major suite to ascribe convincingly the authorship of the latter work to Prelleur.

3.6. Lost and Spurious Concerti

In about 1725, Walsh and Hare published:

> Corelli's XII concertos [Op 6] transpos'd for Flutes, viz., a Fifth, a Sixth, a Consort and Voice Flute, the proper Flute being nam'd to each Concerto and so adapted to the Parts that they perform in Consort with the Violins and other Instruments. Throughout the whole being the first of its kind yet published.

Only fragments of this arrangement survive (none of the recorder parts) and the name of the arranger is not known, but Hawkins suggests that it was Johann Christian Schickhardt.[133]

In 1988 Peter Thalheimer published an edition of a *flauto piccolo* concerto attributed to Handel which was discovered in a manuscript in Rostock. However a further article by the same author in 2000 suggests that the composer was more likely to have been (?Francesco) Montenari.[134] Nikolaj Tarasov, writing in *Windkanal* in 2009, concurs.[135] There are almost certainly further undiscovered works of this genre, and Thalheimer notes that works of Handel were performed on the 'little flute' in the 1720s and 1730s.[136] To date, I have not found any convincing evidence for this practice but it seems a reasonable supposition, given recorder players' propensity for making arrangements.[137]

3.7. Discussion

The descriptive comments on eighteen works for small recorder(s) and strings require an overall analysis of the features which they exhibit in common and of the features in which they differ. The concerti by Babell, Baston and Woodcock are substantially similar in style and may be considered as one group: the Dieupart, Sammartini and the anonymous suite do not fall easily into this pattern.

Harmonically, Babell's, Baston's and Woodcock's concerti conform broadly to the conventions

---

132   In an email, (13 July 2005), Peter Holman commented to me that Add. MS 31453 was 'likely to be by Prelleur because the trumpet works in the same sequence are attributed to Prelleur in a German source'; D–Dl 2709–0–1.

133   'When the flute was an instrument in vogue this was a very common practice [transposition of the recorder parts], Corelli's Concertos had been in like manner fitted for flutes by Schickard of Hamburg, a great performer on, and composer for, that instrument' (Hawkins, *A General History of the Science and Practice of Music*, vol.5, note, p.180.

134   Peter Thalheimer, 'Spurensuche im Repertoire für 'flauto piccolo': Händel oder Montenari?—das ist hier die Frage', *Windkanal*, 2 (2000), 6–10.

135   Tarasov, 'Händel und Blockflöte'.

136   Thalheimer, *ibid*; the *Daily Courant* of 16 May 1717 advertised a benefit concert for Mr. Castelman at the Theatre Royal, Drury Lane, which included a concerto on the little flute by Paisible and 'one entirely new, compos'd by Mr. Handel'.

137   Peter Holman, in conversation with MacMillan in July 2016, suggested that the solo parts in Handel's Concerto Grosso Op.3 no.3 may have been written for the recorder player John Baston and his violinist brother Thomas: examination of the music confirms that the flute (recorder) part would lie comfortably on a fifth or sixth flute.

described by Michael Talbot, modulation being substantially confined to the closely-related keys of the dominant, relative minor and mediant minor (in the major) and to the dominant and relative major in the minor mode. In the major key concerti (fourteen), the slow movement is in the relative minor and five of these conclude on a chord of the dominant. The final movements do not follow any set pattern, and only three are written in specific dance forms. Whereas the concerti published by Walsh conform to a conventional – and fairly consistent – pattern, the Dieupart and Sammartini pieces exhibit more extensive modulation: in the case of the Sammartini, this may perhaps be explained by its later date of composition, although the Dieupart may date from the 1720s. Both men were accomplished composers, whereas Baston and Woodcock are only known for their handful of concerti. Babell, in this respect, was a more significant composer and also a noted harpsichordist, so it is perhaps surprising that his recorder concerti do not show more extensive harmonic development: they may be youthful works. The anonymous suite shows similar conventional harmonisation and orchestration to the 'Walsh' concerti, suggesting a similar date of composition. Orchestrally, the Babell, Baston, and Woodcock concerti exhibit a similar pattern with ripieno violin parts, but these parts are lacking in the Dieupart and Sammartini concerti.

Babell, Baston and Woodcock's concerti rank amongst the first concerti for solo instrument and strings to be published in England, and evidence from concert notices and playbills suggest that they were composed some years before their publication by Walsh and Hare in the late 1720s. Although tuneful, they are harmonically unadventurous and performance (particularly with one-to-a-part strings) would have posed no problems for the audience to hear the solo recorder: small recorders, in this sense, make better concerto instruments than altos. There are no documented performances of the (later) Sammartini concerto although the Dieupart may have been played in London in the 1720s; the A major suite remains in manuscript score.

Chapter 4

Performances and unresolved questions

4.1. Abstract of the chapter

Music is composed to be performed, and the instruments for which it is written and the audiences to whom it is to be played are both of considerable importance to the historian of music, whose brief inevitably combines the disciplines of organology, musicology, and sociology. This chapter examines representative performances of the small flute concerti given between 1717 and 1734 in order to place the works in a context which would have been apparent to both contemporary musicians and their audiences. Final paragraphs summarise the findings of the foregoing chapters, answering questions that may rightly be asked, and noting a number of (at present) unanswered questions.

4.2. Representative performances

The examples cited are not intended as a comprehensive record of all performances of small flute concerti and can only represent the tip of an iceberg: they serve solely to provide an overview of the diversity of performances over a period of almost twenty years. As Stanley Sadie noted 'Concert life in eighteenth-century England as a whole had a variety and vitality to which it would be hard to find a parallel' and commented on the plethora of musical performances (often by amateurs) in provincial towns; more recently, John Brewer wrote 'Most music was played informally in clubs and societies made up by amateur musicians'.[138]

My article in *The Consort* of 2006 noted that, out of twenty-six documented performances of small flute concerti, twenty-one took places in the various theatres. Listed below are ten representative performances to illustrate the scope and variety of performances and venues between 1717 and 1734, after which no public notice of further performances of the concerti appeared.

1.
11 November 1717; Lincoln's Inn Fields Theatre
Love makes a Man
MUSIC A Concerto for the Violin and Flutes, compos'd by John Baston and perform'd by him and his Brother.
DANCING as 22 October.[139]

2.
4 May 1720; Lincoln's Inn Fields Theatre
The Comical History of Don Quixote
'With a Concerto on the Sixth Flute by Mr. Bastion [sic], jr.[140]

3.
16 May 1718; Theatre Royal, Drury Lane
King Henry the IVth.
A Concerto on the little Flute by Paisible, and one intirely [*sic*] new compos'd by Mr Hendel[sic].[141]

---

138   Sadie, 'Concert Life in Eighteenth-Century England'; John Brewer, *The Pleasures of the Imagination* (Abingdon: Routledge, 2013), p.293.

139   *The London Stage* 2, p.468; the concerto may have been for a small recorder or an alto.

140   *The Daily Post*, 4 May 1720.

141   *Daily Courant*, 16 May 1718; James (Jacques) Paisible (*c.*1656–1721) was a French recorder virtuoso who arrived in England in 1673.

4.

14 March 1722; Theatre Royal, Drury Lane

Concert for the benefit of Carbonelli

Three 'entertainments': in the third entertainment (item 4 of 6) 'A New Concerto on Little Flute composed by Woodcocke [sic] and performed by John Baston'.[142]

5.

11 May 1722; Theatre Royal, Drury Lane

Sir Courtly Nice

MUSIC Select Pieces, Particularly a Concerto for the Little Flute composed by Monsieur Dieupart, and performed by Mr Baston and others.[143]

6.

11 May 1722; Little Theatre, Haymarket

Concert, including A Concerto on the Little Flute by Grano.[144]

7.

16 April 1729; Concert at Hickford's Rooms

A Concert for the Benefit of Kytch

Part III included 'Concerto for the Little Flute composed by Babel.'… 'All the Vocal Parts performed by Kytch on the Hautboy, also the Little Flute and Bassoon'.[145]

8.

9 March 1732; Concert in the Great Room at the Three Tuns…

A Concert of Vocal and Instrumental Musick, by the best Masters in which Mr. Schickhard will perform himself, the whole night's entertainment being his own Composition (entirely New) and will consist of the following Pieces, viz.

> 1. […]
> 2. […]
> 3. A Solo for the small Flute and Bass
> 4. […]
> 5. A Trio for the small Flute, Violin, and Bass
> 6. […]
> 7. A Solo for the small Flute and Bass
> 8. […]
> 9. A Concerto for the small Flute, Violins, &c.
> 10. A Solo on the small Flute, with Ecchoes [sic] and Bass
> 12. A concerto for French Horns, Small Flute, Hautboys, Violins, &c.[146]

9.

9 May 1733; Theatre Royal, Drury Lane

Rule a Wife and have a Wife

Concerto on the Little Flute by John Bastion *[sic]*

---

142 *Daily Courant*, 13 March 1722; *Daily Post*, 14 March 1722.

143 *Daily Courant*, 11 May 1722.

144 *The London Stage… Part 2*, p.677; 'By' in this context means 'performed by', not necessarily 'composed by'; John Baptist Grano was a noted trumpeter who was for a time incarcerated in the Debtor's Prison at Marshalsea.

145 *Daily Post*, 11, 14, 15 April 1729.

146 *Daily Post*, 9 March 1732.

This is the last advertised performance by Baston.[147]

10.
8 May 1734; Goodman's Fields Theatre
King Richard the Third
Second music: Concerto of the late Mr Woodcock's on the Little Flute
This is the last advertised English performance of a small flute concerto.[148]

Performances 1, 2, 4, 5 and 9 relate to John Baston, illustrating his career from the first recorded performance of a concerto in 1717 to his final performance in 1733. It is known that he was active from 1709, but these early performances may have been as a 'cellist rather than as a recorder player.[149] They were given at Lincoln's Inn Fields Theatre or the Theatre Royal, Drury Lane, but there is evidence that Baston performed in other venues around London: the collaboration with his brother Thomas is apparent in item 1, when he performed 'A Concerto for the Violin and Flutes, compos'd by John Baston and perform'd by him and his Brother' and that he also played other composer's music is shown in his performance of concerti by Dieupart and by Woodcock in 1722 (4 and 5). All these performances were given in theatres: however, in 1729 the Dutch oboist Jack Kytch (died 1738) performed one of Babell's concerti at Hickford's Rooms (7). This is the only documented performance of a Babell recorder concerto, but Walsh (in the title-page to his publication of Babell's concerti) notes that they 'were 'Perform'd at the theatre with great applause'. Collaborative evidence for this assertion is, at present, lacking. The player and/or composer was not always specified in playbills: for example, the noted recorder player James Paisible played at Drury Lane in 1718 (3) and the trumpeter and flautist John Grano (*p*1692–*a*1748) played an unspecified concerto on the 'Little Flute' at the Little Theatre, Haymarket, in 1722 (6).[150] The German composer and recorder player Johann Christian Schickhardt (*c*.1681–1762) gave a concert at the Three Tuns and Bulls-Head in Cheapside in 1732, the listed music including a concerto for small flute and four other pieces for small flute (8): none of this music has survived, but the description is interesting, for, apart from the concerti and obbligato passages, there appears to be no surviving English music for small recorders dating from the 1730s. A similar situation existed in Continental Europe: apart from Vivaldi's three concerti for sopranino and three concerti for *flauto piccolo* listed in the Breitkopf catalogue of 1763, there are no sonatas or concerti for small recorders.[151]

It appears that the interest in the small flute concerti was waning – as indeed was the popularity of the recorder – by the 1730s, but it is noteworthy that Babell, Baston, and Woodcock's music continued to appear in publishers' catalogues for a further forty years.

4.3. Unresolved questions and conclusion

There remain a number of unsolved mysteries relating to the English small flute concerti, the first being the choice of instruments. There is little doubt that small recorders pose fewer problems of orchestral balance than altos (even when using one-to-a-part strings) so the choice of this size of instrument is entirely comprehensible. What is curious, however, is the particular prominence of the sixth flute, an instrument very rarely encountered in Continental European music of the early

---

147   Arthur H. Scrouten, (ed.), *The London Stage, 1660–1800…Part 3, 1729–1747* (Carbondale: Southern Illinois University Press, 1961), p.298.

148   *The London Stage* 3, p.396.

149   See Chapter 3, section 3.4.

150   The concerto by Handel has not been identified.

151   Barry S. Brook, *The Breitkopf Thematic Catalogue. The Six Parts and Sixteen Supplements, 1762–1787* (New York: Dover Publications, 1966), p.21.

eighteenth century. As I have indicated in Chapter 2, the sixth flute is particularly suited to the sharp keys in which the majority of the concerti are written but very few sixth flutes (of English or continental origin) survive: if there were a plethora of surviving English sixth flutes, the reason for the choice of this instrument would be more apparent. Were the concerti composed in sharp keys to suit this particular recorder, or did the availability of the instrument influence the composer's choice of keys? Only one concerto require the full compass of the recorder (two octaves and a second), and it is worth noting that much English alto recorder music of the period seldom extends above d''', in contrast to the German composers Bach and Telemann, who frequently require the highest register of the recorder. The sopranino was the most frequently assigned octave recorder in English music of the early eighteenth century (particularly as an obbligato instrument, and often played to imitate bird-song) but there are no English concerti for the instrument.

The concerti published by Walsh (Babell, Baston, and Woodcock) conform to a similar style of composition, with simple harmonic development, extensive passage-work in the solo line and occasional prominent solo violin parts. Most of the recorder parts are within the ability of a competent amateur player (as are the string parts) but there is no convincing evidence for amateur performance: however, the continued publication by Walsh and his successors suggests a reasonable market for the concerti. Woodcock, as an amateur player, may have composed for like-minded friends, whereas Baston would have composed for his own use in the theatre. The greater complexity of the Sammartini concerto may well be explained both by its later date of composition (although this cannot be established with certainty) and the prominence of its composer as a particularly gifted woodwind player.

It is also appropriate to consider why these works are essentially an English phenomenon. Public concerts and theatre entertainments formed a background to the musical life of London in the early eighteenth century whereas in Europe, small courts with their private bands and exclusive musical culture dominated the scene. I have shown above that the small flute concerti were performed in theatres, concert rooms and taverns, places all accessible to the public, again in contrast to European practice. The long evenings of spoken drama in the theatre were interspersed with 'light relief' in the form of *entr'acte* episodes, in which the concerti (particularly Baston's compositions) were popular. I conclude that one of the prime reasons for the peculiarly-English small flute concerti relates to the musical and theatrical environment pertaining in London in the early eighteenth century

Documented performances of the concert were given over a period of about twenty years in London theatres and concert halls but, after the early 1730s, the pieces faded into oblivion. The concerti were undoubtedly popular in their hey-day and would have provided a welcome break from the spoken word during a long evening in the theatre but tastes in music — as in painting, fashion, politics and religion, change. Perhaps as a twentieth century parallel, it is appropriate to recall that the particularly influential pop group *The Beatles* were only active for ten years! The recorder was declining in popularity by the third decade of the eighteenth century: Babell and Woodcock had died in the 1720s and Baston passed away around 1739. Happily the small flute concerti have been resurrected from their historical oblivion, and the pleasure with which they are received by twenty-first century audiences is surely a mirror of their popularity in the early eighteenth century.

The small flute concerti may not rank with the greatest achievements of the days of Bach, Handel, Telemann and Vivaldi but as a uniquely English contribution to the history of the recorder they represent a veritable oyster of fine – if small – pearls.

Appendix 1.

Extant eighteenth-century English octave recorders

1.

Description	Sopranino
Maker	Benjamin Hallett, London
Date	*fl a*1736– *p*1753
Location	NL-Amsterdam: Brüggen private collection
Lowest note	f"
Pitch	a'=405
Length	259.8mm
Pieces	3
Material	ivory
Mounts	unmounted
Stamp	on all three joints: HALLETT
Source	Lander[152]

2.

Description	sixth flute
Maker	Thomas Stanesby, sr., London
Date	1668–1734, *fl*1691–1733/34
Location	US–DC–Washington: Dayton C Miller Flute Collection
Collection ID	DCM 1214
Lowest note	d"
Pitch	a'=410
Length	303mm
Pieces	3
Material	ivory
Mounts	unmounted
Stamp	on all three joints: T/STANESBY/ (sunburst): also '6' on foot-joint
Source	Lander, Young[153]
Provenance	ex W Howard Head
Notes	some damage to foot and lip; '6' on the foot-joint is a pitch mark

3.

Description	Sixth flute
Maker	Thomas Stanesby, jr., London
Date	1692–1734, *fl*1713–1754
Location	NL–Amsterdam: Brüggen private collection
Lowest note	d"
Pitch	a'=429
Length	308mm
Pieces	3
Material	ivory
Mounts	unmounted

---

152 N.S. Lander, 'Instruments' *Recorder Home Page*, (1996–2016), http://www.recorderhomepage.net/instruments, (accessed 14 December 2015).

153 Philip T.Young, *4900 Historical Woodwind Instruments* (London: Tony Bingham, 1993).

Stamp	STANESBY/IUNIOR/D; cherub's head engraved on head, grapevine on body
Source	Lander, Young
Provenance	ex Hunt
Notes	an elaborately-decorated ivory recorder.

4.

Description	soprano (fifth flute)
Maker	Thomas Stanesby, jr., London
Date	1692–1734, fl1713–54
Location	A–Vienna: Clemencic private collection
Lowest note	c"
Material	ivory
Mounts	unmounted
Stamp	?
Source	Lander, Young
Provenance	ex Baines ex Galpin
Notes	no other data available

5.

Description	soprano (fifth flute)
Maker	Thomas Stanesby, jr., London
Date	1692–1734, fl1713–54
Location	J-Tokyo: Iino private collection
Lowest note	c"
Material	ivory
Mounts	gold
Stamp	STANESBY/IUNIOR/6. Gold points inlaid in ivory on all three joints
Source	Lander, Young
Notes	no other data available

6.

Description	soprano (fifth flute)
Maker	John Just Schuchart, London
Date	1695–1758, fl1731–53
Location	US–OH–Cincinnati: Art Museum
Collection ID	1914.140
Length	355mm
Material	boxwood
Mounts	horn
Stamp	IuI/SCHUCHART/2-headed spread eagle
Source	Lander, Young, collection curator[154]
Provenance	ex Taphouse
Notes	no other data available

7.

Description	Soprano
Maker	Benjamin Hallett, London
Date	fl a1736–p1753
Location	USA–SD–Vermillion: Shrine to Music Museum
Collection ID	4825

---

154   lisa.delong@cincyart.com: email to MacMillan 26 February 2016.

Lowest note	c"
Pitch	a'=396
Length	368mm
Pieces	3
Material	boxwood
Mounts	unmounted
Stamp	on all three joints: 4/HALLETT
Source	Lander
Provenance	ex Spiegl: ex Higbee-Abbott-Zylstra
Notes	The length of the instrument and the mark '4' suggests it is a fourth flute

8.

Description	fourth flute
Maker	Peter Jaillard Bressan, London
Date	fl1688–1730
Location	GB–Oxford: Bate Collection, University of Oxford
Collection ID	0109
Lowest note	b-flat'
Pitch	a'=430 (see notes)
Length	367mm
Pieces	3
Material	stained boxwood
Mounts	unmounted
Stamp	on head: PuI/BRESSAN/(rose)/4
	on body: between holes 2 and 3: 4
	between holes 3 and 4 as on head
	on foot: as on head
Source	examined May 2014
Provenance	ex Hunt
Notes	The foot has been slightly altered to raise the pitch of the instrument to a'=430; in playing condition. Byrne (1983), however, reports that the instrument was three-quarters the size of a treble, but has been shortened by about 12mm at the upper tenon.[155]

9.

Description	fourth flute
Maker	Thomas Stanesby, jr., London
Date	1692-1734, fl1713-1754
Location	US – anonymous
Lowest note	b-flat'
Material	boxwood
Mounts	unmounted
Stamp	head only: STANESBY/JUNIOR/4
Source	Lander: Young
Notes	head joint only. '4' is a pitch mark

155 Maurice Byrne, 'Pierre Jaillard Bressan', *Galpin Society Journal*, 36 (1983), 2–28.

10.

Description	soprano recorder
Maker	Benjamin Hallett, London
Date	*fl a*1736–*p*1753
Location	GB–Torquay: Torquay Museum
Collection ID	V4608
Length	333mm
Pieces	3
Material	rosewood
Mounts	ivory mouthpiece sleeve and upper ring
Stamp	on head: HALLETT
Source	museum staff
Notes	listed in an early edition of Langwill's Index

11.

Description	Soprano recorder
Maker	John Mason, London
Date	*fl a*1754–*p*56
Location	GB–Brighton: Brighton Museum and Art Gallery
Collection ID	R5773/119
Pitch	c"
Length	384mm (sounding length 287mm)
Materials	boxwood
	Stamp on all three joints: MASON / 5
Provenance	ex Albert C Spencer
Notes	A soprano recorder dating from the mid-eighteenth century; no other recorders by this maker are reported; the tone-holes are undercut, with some wear on the thumb-hole; the instrument is slightly warped; the foot-joint appears as though it was made from a different wood, but it bears the same stamp as the other joints and a crack in the joint has been glued; it is otherwise in good conservation condition; the mark 'MASON' is not reported in the *New Langwill Index*, and the figure '5' indicates a fifth flute. Few soprano recorders from this period are extant, and Mason is known primarily as a flute-maker.

Appendix 2

The small flute concerti: bibliographic data

1.

Babell's/CONCERTOS/in 7 Parts:/The first four for VIOLINS and one small Flute/and the two last for VIOLINS and two FLUTES./The proper Flute being nam'd to each CONCERTO. Compos'd by the Late/Mr. WILLm. BABELL./Performed at the Theatre with great applause./Opera Terza.

Composer	William Babell (c.1690–1723)
Date	c.1715: published 1726
Publisher	Walsh and Hare
Location	GB–HAdolmetsch II C39. 1–7; GB–Y 195–197 (printed music).
Notes	RISM B6; for comments on date of composition, see Chapter 3.

2.

Six/CONCERTOS/in Six Parts/for VIOLINS and FLUTES/viz. a Fifth, Sixth and Consort Flute./The Proper Flute being nam'd to each/CONCERTO/Compos'd by/Mr/John Baston.

Composer	John Baston (died c.1739)
Date	c.1715–29: published 1729
Publisher	Walsh and Hare
Location	GB–Lbl i.53.
Notes	RISM B1240

3.

XII CONCERTOS/in Eight Parts/The first three for/VIOLINS and one Small FLUTE/The Second three for/VIOLINS and two Small FLUTES/The third three for/VIOLINS & One GERMAN FLUTE/and the three last for/VIOLINS/& one HOBOY/The proper Flute Being nam'd to each Concert /Compos'd by ROBERT WOODCOCK.

Composer	Robert Woodcock (1690–1728)
Date	1720s: published 1728
Publisher	Walsh and Hare
Location	GB–Lbl i.25; GB–CDu 3.56 (Mackworth); S–Skma FbO_R; S–L Englehart 202 (concerti 8, 9, 10 missing); S–L 696, 697a (concerto 4 only).
Notes	RISM W1862; the authorship of these concerti is discussed in Chapter 3.

4.

CONCERTO/à 5./Flautino,et, 4 Violons./Mons: Dieupart

Composer	Charles Dieupart (c.1667–c.1740)
Date	1720s
Publisher	in MS
Location	D–Dl Mus.2174–0–1
Notes	RISM 212001265; in manuscript; for related title-page in another hand, see Chapter 3.

5.

Concerto a piu Istrumenti per la Fluta. Di. Giusep.° St. Martini.

Composer	Giuseppe Sammartini (1695 – 1750)
Date	c.1730
Publisher	in MS
Location	S-Skma FbO-R
Notes	Not published in C18

6.

Allemanda, andante and minuet

Composer	Anonymous
Date	early C18
Publisher	unpublished
Location	GB–Lbl Add. MS 31453.

Bibliography

Primary sources

Bibliographic data relating to the concerti is given in Appendix 2.

Charles Burney, *A General History of Music from the Earliest Ages to the Present Period*, [1789], ed. by Frank Mercer, 2 vols., (New York: Dover, 1957).

A Catalogue of the Vocal and Instrumental Music Printed for, and sold by, William Randall, Successor to the late Mr. John Walsh, in Catherine-Street in the Strand for the year 1776.

John Essex, *The Young Ladies Conduct: or, Rules for Education* (London: 1722).

John Hawkins, *A General History of the Science and Practice of Music* (London: printed for T. Payne & Son, 1776).

Samuel Hellier, 'A Catalogue of Musicall Instruments', *Galpin Society Journal*, 18 (1965), 5–6.

John Wilson (ed.), *Roger North on Music* (London: Novello, 1959).

John Simpson (publisher), *THE DELIGHTFUL/Pocket Companion/for the/GERMAN FLUTE... PRINTED for/& sold by John Simpson* (London: John Simpson, 1745),

William Tans'ur, *A New Musical Grammar: or, the Harmonical Spectator. Containing All the useful Theoretical, Practical, and Technical Parts of Musick...* (for the author, 1746).

Secondary sources

Denis Arnold, 'Charity Music in 18th-Century Dublin, *Galpin Society Journal*, 11 (1968), 162–174.

Anthony Baines, 'James Talbot's Manuscript', *Galpin Society Journal*, 1 (1948), 9–26.

Anthony Baines, *Woodwind Instruments and Their History* (London: Faber and Faber, corrected 3rd. edn, 1977, repr. New York: Dover Publications, 1991).

The Blackwell History of Music in Britain: The Eighteenth Century, ed. by H. Diack Johnstone and Roger Fiske (Oxford: Basil Blackwell, 1990).

John Brewer, *The Pleasures of the Imagination* (Abingdon: Routledge, 2013).

Barry S. Brook, *The Breitkopf Thematic Catalogue. The Six Parts and Sixteen Supplements, 1762–1787* (New York: Dover Publications, 1966).

The Cambridge Companion to the Recorder, ed. by John Mansfield Thomson (Cambridge: Cambridge University Press, 1995).

Adam Carse, *Musical Wind Instruments* (New York: 1939, repr. Da Capo Press, 1956).

Robert Donington, *The Interpretation of Early Music* (London: Faber and Faber, 1975).

Robert Elkin, *The Old Concert Rooms of London* (London: Edward Arnold, 1955).

Roger Fiske, *English Theatre Music in the Eighteenth Century* (Oxford: 2nd. edn, Oxford University Press, 1986).

Zöe Franklin, 'William Babel's [*sic*] *Concertos in Seven Parts*, *The Consort*, 63 (2007), 62–73.

Gerald Gifford and Terence Best, 'Babell, William' *Grove Music Online, Oxford Music Online*, http:// www.oxfordmusiconline.com (Oxford: Oxford University Press, 2007–2016, accessed 19 August 2015).

Richard Griscom and David Lasocki, *The Recorder. A Research and Information Guide* (New York: 3rd. edn, Routledge, 2012).

Eric Halfpenny, 'The English Baroque Treble Recorder', *Galpin Society Journal*, 9 (1956), 82–90.

Peter Holman and Richard Maunder, 'The Accompaniment of Concertos in 18th-Century England', *Early Music*, 28/4 (2000), 37–50.

Charles Humphries and William C. Smith, *Music Publishing in the British Isles* (London: Cassell, 1954).

Edgar Hunt, *The Recorder and Its Music* (Hebden Bridge: 3rd., edn, Peacock Press, 2002).

Arthur Hutchings, *The Baroque Concerto* (London: 2nd. edn., Faber and Faber, 1972).

The London Stage 1660–1800. A Calendar of Plays, Entertainments and Afterpieces, Together with Casts, Box-receipts and Contemporary Comment Compiled from the Playbills, Newspapers and Theatrical Diaries of the Period, 5 parts (Carbondale: Southern Illinois University Press, 1960–1968); Part 1: 1660–1700, ed. by William Van Lennep, (1960); Part 2: 1700-1729, ed. by Emmett L. Avery, (1960); Part 3, ed. by Arthur H. Scrouton, (1961).

The New Langwill Index, ed. by William Waterhouse (London: Tony Bingham, 1993).

David Lasocki, 'New Light on Eighteenth-Century English Woodwind Makers', *Galpin Society Journal*, 63 (2010), 73–142.

_____, and Anthony Rowland-Jones, 'The Eighteenth-Century Recorder Concerto' in *The Cambridge Companion to the Recorder*, ed. by John Mansfield Thomson (Cambridge: Cambridge University Press, 1995).

_____, and Helen Neate, 'The Life and Works of Robert Woodcock, 1690–1728', *American Recorder*, 24/3 (1988), 92–104.

_____, 'Amateur Recorder playing in Renaissance and Baroque England', *American Recorder*, 40/1 (1999), 15–18.

Douglas MacMillan, 'The Descant Recorder in the Early Eighteenth Century', *Recorder and Music*, 7/1 (1981), 12–13.

_____, 'The Small Flute Concerto in 18th-Century England', *The Consort*, 62 (2006), 91–106.

_____, The Sopranino Recorder in England, 1750 – 1800', *A Handbook for Studies in 18th.-Century Music,* 22 (2018), 19 – 25.

Sybil Marcuse, *A Survey of Musical Instruments* (New York: Harper & Row, 1975).

Richard Maunder, *The Scoring of Baroque Concertos* (Woodbridge: The Boydell Press, 2004).

Lenz Meierott, *Die geschichtliche Entwicklung der kleinen Flötentypen und ihre Verwendung in der Musik des17.und 18.Jahrhunderts* (Tutzing: Schneider, 1974).

Susi Möhlmeier and Frédéric Thouvenot, 'Introduction to Jean Marc Fuzeau's facsimile edition of John Baston's *Six Concertos (1729),* ed. Jean Marc Fuzeau (Courlay; Fouzeau, 1997).

Brian Priestman, 'An Introduction to the Loeillets', *The Consort*, 11 (1954), 18–26.

Stanley Sadie, 'Concert Life in Eighteenth-Century England', *Proceedings of the Royal Musical Association* 85 (1958 – 59), 17.

Frederico Maria Sardelli, *Vivaldi's Music for Flute and Recorder*, trans. Michael Talbot (Aldershot: Ashgate, 2007).

Fiona Smith, 'Original Performing Material for Concerted Music in England, *c.*1660–1800', PhD diss., University of Leeds, 2014.

Michael Talbot, 'The Concerto Allegro in the Early Eighteenth Century' *Music and Letters*, 52/1, (1971), 8–18.

Michael Tilmouth, 'A Calendar of References to Music in Newspapers published in London and the Provinces (1660–1719)', *Royal Musical Association Research Chronicle*, 1 (1961), 1–107.

The Twenty-Second Volume of the Walpole Society. Vertue Note Books, Volume III (Oxford: Oxford University Press, 1934),

Christopher Welch, *Six Lectures on the Recorder and other Flutes in Relation to Literature* (London: Oxford University Press, 1911), n4, pp.150–3.

Jerry White, *London in the Eighteenth Century* (London: Vintage Books, 2013).

Websites

Sales of flutes and recorders
David Lasocki, 'Lessons from inventories and sales of flutes and recorders', www.instantharmony.net/Music/lessons-from-inventories.pdf./ (accessed 11–17 March 2014).

Small flute concerti
David Lasocki. *"Recorder".Grove Music Online. Oxford Music Online.* Oxford University Press, accessed 13 July 2017, http://www.oxfordmusiconline.com/subscriber/article/grove/music/23022/.

Grove Music Online
http://www.oxfordmusiconline.com/subscriber/article/grove/music/ (multiple accessions, 2014–17).

The Recorder Home Page
N.S.Lander, 'Instruments', The Recorder Home Page (1996–2017), www.recorderhomepage.net/instruments/, (accessed 17 July 2017).

Musical Instrument Museums Online (MIMO)
www.mimo-international.com/. (accessed 17 July 2017).

Index

www.ingramcontent.com/pod-product-compliance
Lightning Source LLC
Chambersburg PA
CBHW060901090426
42738CB00023B/3483